SKETCHING STUFF

Stories Sketched From Life

CHARLIE O'SHIELDS

doodlewash.com

Copyright © 2018 Charlie O'Shields.

All rights reserved. No part of this book may be reproduced in any form or by any electronic or mechanical means, including information storage and retrieval systems, without written permission from the author, except for the use of brief quotations in a book review. For more information, address: letspaint@doodlewash.com.

DOODLEWASH is a registered trademark of Storywize, LLC.
All Rights Reserved.

ISBN 978-0-9600219-1-8 (Paperback)
ISBN 978-0-9600219-0-1 (Hardcover)

The events and conversations in this book have been set down to the best of the author's mental ability and memory, such as it is, and some names and details have been changed to protect the privacy of individuals.

Illustrations by Charlie O'Shields
Cover Design by Charlie O'Shields

First Edition
November 2018

Published by *Doodlewash Books,* an imprint of Doodlewash

www.doodlewash.com

This book is dedicated to my little immediate family, which consists of a lovely Parisian fellow named Philippe and a lovable, yet demanding, little basenji dog named Phineas. Together, they add more joy to my life than I thought was possible and inspire me each day to keep chasing crazy new ideas.
And also, my mom, for teaching me to focus on the laughter and fun in life, and always encouraging me to follow my dreams.

ACKNOWLEDGMENTS

A huge thanks to every member of the Doodlewash® online community for the constant inspiration and particularly those of you who comment on my posts and encourage me to write more. My mother always said, "don't encourage him," but I'm thrilled that you didn't listen to her and did so anyway (she was kidding by the way… I think…). It really means the world to me, and is the very reason you're now holding this book in your hands. I assumed hands, as I wasn't sure how else you'd do it, but if you've figured out another way, then that's perfectly awesome!

CONTENTS

THE JOURNEY BEGINS

1. Once Upon A Time — 3
2. Cast Of Characters — 7
3. The Casual Artist — 11
4. Sketching Memories — 15
5. My Watercolory Book — 18

DAYS TO CELEBRATE

1. World Cliché Day — 31
2. World Television Day — 34
3. National Apple Cider Day — 37
4. Area Code Day — 39
5. Absurdity Day — 42

CABINET OF CURIOSITIES

1. Magic Lantern — 47
2. Calling Mom — 50
3. Swatch — 53
4. Blue Yellow Macaw — 55
5. Neighborhood Cat — 58

CHILDHOOD FAVORITES

1. Oompa-Loompas — 63

2. Lawn Darts	66
3. Rock 'Em Sock 'Em Robots	68
4. Fish In A Bowl	70
5. Barrel Of Monkeys	73
6. Troll Dolls	75

WHEN THE MUSIC PLAYS

1. My Favorite Song	79
2. Playing The Violin	82
3. That Time I Played Guitar	85
4. Bears, Pears, And Dirty Dancing	88
5. Lost In A Song	91
6. When The Music Plays	94

THOSE FURRY FRIENDS

1. Playing With a Pet	99
2. My First Dog	102
3. Sparky The Hamster	105
4. Sometimes, You Get Lucky	108
5. If I Could Have A Kitten	111
6. Duckie	114

LAUGHING UNTIL IT HURTS

1. Laughing Until It Hurts	119
2. Traveling By Plane	122
3. Pancakes For Breakfast	126
4. The Sweat Bee	129
5. Making Sno-cones	132
6. Waiting For the Bubble To Pop	135

WHEN WE WERE KIDS

1. Little Charlie — 141
2. Eating Like a Kid Again — 144
3. My First Little Bike — 147
4. Candy Day — 150
5. Rubber Duckie, You're The One — 153
6. When There Were Dragons — 156

LITTLE LIFE LESSONS

1. Shades of Blue — 161
2. The Quilt My Grandmother Made For Me — 164
3. Journey To A Distant Land — 167
4. Life In Jeans — 170
5. Simple Things — 173
6. Message In A Bottle — 176

HALLOWEEN HIJINKS

1. Spooky Spider — 181
2. The Raven — 184
3. A Witch's Broomstick — 187
4. Pumpkins In The Hay — 190
5. The Invisible Man — 193
6. Contemplating The Moon — 196

SKETCHING ALL THE WAY

1. World Dream Day — 201
2. My Little Kitchen Travel Palette — 204
3. How To Build A Daily Art Habit — 207

FOR THE LOVE OF FAMILY

1. Where The Wild Flowers Grow — 225
2. Grandparent's Day — 228
3. Thanksgiving In Paris — 231
4. Country Music Day — 234
5. World Kindness Day — 237
6. When He Was A Puppy — 241

HAPPY HOLIDAY MOMENTS

1. Sledding Down A Hill — 247
2. Two Turtle Doves — 250
3. Men In Boots — 253
4. Silver Bells — 256
5. The Gingerbread Man — 258
6. A Snow Day — 261
7. A Letter To Santa — 264

About the Author — 269

THE JOURNEY BEGINS

Every story has a beginning… but when you call it an "Introduction" people tend to skip that bit. So, please read on, as this first section is truly the best place to start.

ONCE UPON A TIME

There once was a little boy, who had a seemingly limitless imagination, on a quest for knowledge. Every trip he would take with his mother would turn into a field trip and an opportunity to discover new things, even if it was just a visit to the local library.

Years would pass, and this boy would grow up, as boys are prone to do, but that spirit never died.

Yep, I'm that little boy, both then and now. I still yearn for knowledge and experiences that let me discover new things. I still happily question the world around me and never simply accept what I'm told as fact. I've always loved making things, but for many years, my various jobs along the way took precedence in my life. I was so focused on doing a good *job* that I didn't often take the time to be good to myself. To let myself play a bit and enjoy life as I used to in the past.

When I started sketching and painting in July of 2015, I felt like that kid again for the first time in years. And rather than approach my new discovery as an adult would, I just kept letting that little boy guide me through each step. Why am I telling you all of this? Well, I've learned that my approach was the often missing ingredient to many of the things I've attempted in my life. I've tried a thousand different things, but many simply faded like a fad, never to be attempted again. Yet, for over three years now, I've dutifully shown up to sketch and write *every single day*.

My writing consists of musings on everyday life more than specific art techniques. All of the best techniques in the world won't help us become better at something, if we don't do it on a regular basis. It's the *doing* that helps us improve each day and feel great about ourselves in the process. Okay, some days are better than others, but the collection of days spent pursuing a passion always creates a sense of joy in the end.

THE JOURNEY BEGINS

This book is a jumble of stories about my own life, thoughts on fads and trends, and other perfectly random things that popped to mind. Or, so it might seem. In truth, everything I talk about has a very simple common theme meant to inspire the creativity in all of us:

Love life, and everything you choose to *do* while living it.

That's really it. It's what that little boy taught me. He didn't feel constrained with rules and expectations, or if he did, he could ignore them easily enough and go right on playing. That's the spirit we need if we want to become truly creative people. I've heard it said that creativity loves constraints because it's how you know when you've broken through the norm and discovered something totally new.

Though most books have a rule about starting at the beginning and working your way forward, this book is free from those constraints. You can read these stories in any order that you choose. Pick one at random on a day when you feel a bit down on yourself or think your creative light is starting to dim. Hopefully, these stories will remind you of all that's good in the world and make the rest of your day positive, or ensure you have lovely dreams.

And there's really nothing better in the world than a good dream.

CAST OF CHARACTERS

Of the various cast members you might find mentioned in this little book, two of the main players deserve a bit of backstory to help you understand things. In case you choose to read the remainder of this book in a random order, which I highly recommend.

My little immediate family consists of my husband Philippe who was born and raised in Paris, France and a willful basenji, named Phineas, who was found wandering the tough streets of Topeka, Kansas. I'm not really sure those streets are tough at all, but it sounds more fun to say it that way.

I discovered Phineas in a local shelter, shortly after he arrived there. His fur was coarse and would nearly cut your hand if you tried to pet him. I wanted a basenji, but I remembered them being softer than that, so I expressed a bit of hesitation. Apparently seeing my hesitation, Phineas immediately jumped into my lap, spinning as he did so, and landed on his back with his feet in the air. It was so impossibly cute and looking into those brown eyes, I was immediately smitten. So, he came home with me that very day, and over the next few weeks was restored to a soft, beautiful, brindle dog with *way* too much energy.

Just a few months later, I met Philippe online, as that's really the only way to meet someone who lives over 4,500 miles away from you. We chatted and became friends, but I never imagined that we'd actually end up together. The whole idea seemed a bit too far-fetched and impossible. It was a full year and a half later before we would actually meet in person in Chicago. And nearly another year after that before he would visit myself and Phineas in Kansas City.

I attempted a sketch of Philippe once, from a photo on that first trip here, but it looks absolutely nothing like him as I'm rubbish at sketching humans. Suffice it to say, he does indeed have a beard, but the likeness ends there. Images of Phineas are more on point as I'm much better at sketching animals.

Throughout this early courtship, I still found it difficult to believe we'd manage to end up on the same continent, but life has a way of simply working out sometimes when you continue to have a bit of hope. He was a PhD research scientist, there happened to be a world-renown research institute in my city, and he found a job working there.

We were later married on a rooftop in Los Angeles with no audience whatsoever, except for our officiant and a waiter who gave us a couple of glasses of complimentary champagne. Our honeymoon was the next day as VIP guests at Universal Studios, riding rides and behaving like children and it was a total blast. We said at the time we'd take a proper honeymoon at some point, but that hasn't happened yet. And truly, we still rather enjoyed that one so it hasn't felt particularly necessary.

If you're wondering, my French is extremely poor and though I'm able to read at a child's level, I can't make out most of what is being said. When we visit family there, I spend most of my visit willing my brain to be smarter and straining my ears to pick up bits of dialogue. Actually learning to speak French properly in on my bucket list, so here's hoping I live for quite a long time as I'll definitely need it. I took Spanish in high school, but in my defense, I had no idea I would marry a French man years later. Yet, the best lived life is the one you simply can't plan in advance.

It was actually Philippe who decided to try watercolor painting one weekend back in July, 2015. He brought home some paints and sat down outside on the terrace to try them. It looked like fun, so I asked him for a piece of paper. Looking back, it was all just a lark at first, but it ignited a creative passion in me that I haven't felt in years. I would never have imagined back then that I would go on to create over 1,300 sketches, build a community of watercolor enthusiasts, create a podcast, and assemble this book.

And I'm grateful each day for the support I've received from Philippe on this journey. By that, I mostly mean treating even my craziest of ideas as though they were simply what was meant to happen next. It takes a very special person to believe in someone else's dreams.

I've not worked out whether Phineas actually cares or not, and I suspect he thinks that what I'm doing with my life is rather silly. After all, why on earth would I bother doing anything at all when there's a lovely bed to enjoy?

THE CASUAL ARTIST

When I first began this art journey, I was perfectly overwhelmed with everything going on around me. Lots of people were doing amazing things with pen and ink and watercolor, creating perfectly incredible sketches and awe-inspiring paintings. I tried full paintings of scenes when I began, but soon discovered that my greatest joy came from just sketching bits of stuff. I was simply on a path to learn and enjoy a fun hobby after work.

Today, that hasn't changed. There was a time when I worried that I should have some other goal in mind. That if this was indeed an art journey, then the end of the path must mean that I would become a professional artist. That I would attend art shows and sell my work and become an art teacher like so many wonderful teachers I was learning from at the time. But the one thing I've learned about *any* creative journey is that there's no one-size-fits-all model. There's not a specific way you are required to go and it's often more fun to forge your own path.

My paintings were nothing a gallery would ever accept and I simply didn't care. And, soon, I realized I wasn't a painter at all, so I didn't really have to worry about that. I'm more of an illustrator, and what I enjoy most is writing and illustrating the little stories that I tell. This book is chock full of those stories, along with the various illustrations that popped up along the way.

If I felt like talking about grocery store sushi, then that's what appeared on the page that day. And I rather liked this little piece of art, but fully realize it won't create a line around the corner of people asking for signed prints. It was just fun to make and fit my story perfectly!

Yet, even saying illustrator evokes the notion that this is something I do as a full-time job and that hasn't happened yet either. So, I simply like to think of myself as a "casual artist" instead. It's roughly the equivalent of an armchair quarterback who shouts commands at the screen while watching a football game on television. Though he isn't truly playing the sport, that fact does nothing to diminish his thrill and enjoyment of it. And I've never been good at sports so I've no idea why I landed on that particular analogy, but it's the first one that came to mind.

The point is, whenever we try to do something creative, it's always pure enjoyment when we begin. There's nobody to compare ourselves to in that moment. And we can't even compare ourselves to *ourselves* because we've *only just begun*. But as we move along the road and create more things, the inner critic pops up to tell us that what we made is awful or not as good as something we made before that.

Yet, for a casual artist like me, none of that applies. It's a hobby, a love, and journey that I've happily embarked upon, simply for the sheer pleasure of *doing* it. Along the way, I've sold a few prints and tote bags, made a couple of books, and had an illustration appear on a candle to eliminate dog odor. And, for me, it's been a blast! I'm just thrilled when anyone likes my work enough to spend a bit of money on purchasing something where it appears. And thanks, by the way, for purchasing this book!

Though I may one day still teach, when I'm done with the wonderful process of learning, I'm quite content with where my journey has lead me. And my single hope in everything I do is to inspire others to start and stick with their *own* creative journey by focusing on the *reason* they started it in the first place.

If there's something creative that *you* love to do, or something you've always wanted to try. DO it! And if it turns out that you *love* doing it, then, just keep right on *doing* it no matter what happens next. I make it all sound so easy because it actually *is* ridiculously easy. There are a hundred books on how to unleash your creativity and how to create art, but this isn't one of those.

This little book is simply about life. My life and stories, that I hope will inspire you on *your* creative life journey. The kind of stories filled with hope and positive thinking meant to put you in a happy mindset and summon your inner child. So you are free to enjoy your own *natural* creativity and all of the many wonders that it can bring.

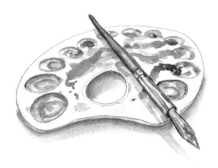

SKETCHING MEMORIES

From the moment I first began sketching, I was drawn to writing about things from my past. Perhaps, it's the calm and wonderful act of creating art that sends me back in time to simpler moments. Or, perhaps, it's just my inner child demanding some attention again. Either way, many of my stories take place decades ago, when they are not simply bits of funny trivia from the crazy world we inhabit. This means, that this book is my memoir as well.

Had I actually set out to write a memoir, I would have gone weak in the knees wondering what the heck to include or how to do it properly. Thankfully, that didn't happen, and, as usual, I did things my own way and gave up on doing them properly at all. Interestingly, this is definitely the best memoir I could have hoped to write. One that's fits my actual crazy personality even in the structure itself. By that I mean, of course, the complete lack of structure.

This book can be read from beginning to end or from the end back to the beginning. There's no particular order of things, though Halloween does indeed come several page numbers before the holiday season. That's about as linear as things occur here, but since you're *also* a creative person, I'm guessing you won't mind.

And this is precisely how memory works in the first place. It's bits of things popping to mind and mixing with other things. Many of my memories are based on stories told by my family and what I recall most from those. But, I'm quite certain that each one is an image of pure *truth*, even if it lacks the documentary precision of a photograph.

Along the way, my writing began to mimic and harmonize with my own loose sketching style. It's bits of musings quickly sketched as they come to mind. Editors everywhere are likely shuddering at this point, but for me, I prefer to write like I'm just sitting down for a nice little chat.

I'm sure a proper writer would have taken the time to change the order of nearly all of the words so that they would appear in a precise and melodic fashion. But, if I talked to you like that while we were having that cup of coffee, you'd think I was losing my mind. And I don't really know how to write that way, so simply typing as I go was the best solution.

And the combination seems like a better fit. My sketches are all created in ink, so there's no eraser. Overusing my delete key might give the writing an unfair advantage. Or, perhaps not. I've always been at my best when I'm not worrying about what I'm doing and simply getting on with the act of *doing* it in the first place. In many ways, I think we all are. And, truly, I'm just as surprised as you are as to what ends up appearing on the page. That's all part of the fun!

MY WATERCOLORY BOOK

As painting mediums go, watercolor is one of the least messy by far. It's easy to use, compact to store, and simple to clean up. That said, I've managed to drip paint on my jeans, and, more than once, I've reached for my drinking glass only to realize I was about to drink out of my muddy mixing cup instead. And that doesn't even begin to count the number of times I've ruined my coffee or a lovely glass of wine by accidentally dunking my brush into it.

My painting style is literally like a child with finger paints who's just eaten an entire plate of cookies and is still buzzing from the sugar high. Don't get me wrong, I started by using masking tape to tape off areas and had all of my paints lined up in perfect order. I would have my clean water and dirty water in place to play by all of the rules my talented instructors had taught me. As I moved forward, however, I switched back again to gleefully popping open my palette of colors and diving in without a plan in mind and things got messy.

Why on earth would I do something like that? Well, I was finding myself losing steam. I was feeling like the correct process had become such a "process" that it was growing a bit tedious. It took extra time that I didn't have, bored me during some moments, and threatened to make me skip a day rather than deal with it all. Don't get me wrong, there's a wonderful and well-vetted process for producing beautiful transparent watercolor paintings. But, as I mentioned, I'm *not* a painter, I'm an illustrator and doodler, and following a process that didn't apply to what I was actually creating was the *real* culprit.

My personal breakthrough came when I reminded myself I wasn't making traditional paintings. I was simply taking my drawings and making them "watercolory." Another term I coined, like doodlewash, but only in my head and this is the first time I've ever mentioned it in print. In my mind, I thought of my sketchbooks as "watercolory books." I would make an initial ink drawing and then use watercolor to quickly finish the sketch and create an illusion of dimension and form.

Though certainly, this involved adding lovely color, color illustrations are prohibitively expensive in printed books, so I wasn't sure how to create a printed version of this one. Then I saw one of my sketches in grayscale and the answer was clear. Watercolor is so amazing in its properties that it just looks really cool, no matter what, even in black and white. And the little kid in me loves the fact that these now perfectly resemble the little illustrations of my favorite chapter books when I was younger. Perhaps, subconsciously, that's what I was creating all along, as my inner child simply insists on doing things *his* way most of the time.

My owl sketch before and after becoming "watercolory"

And I'm thrilled with my "watercolory" ways and wouldn't change a thing. If it sounds fun to make your own drawings and color them, just like you did when you were a little kid, then I do hope you'll try it as well! We've all doodled in the margins of our notebooks when we were young, so the foundation is already there. Though, I definitely recommend drawing classes as a good way to start.

I took drawing classes in college and they were my favorite classes of all. Actually those courses and my creative writing classes were really the only classes I truly enjoyed during my college years. And algebra is still a bit of a mystery to me, but thankfully, I've never had the need to ever use it in real life. Looking back, where I've ended up today is probably not too surprising. It's funny how much easier it is to recognize the obvious in hindsight.

Life is never sweeter than when we are doing something that we love most. This often seems like a luxury many days, when our task lists start to grow with all of the tedious adult things we have to do in life. So, I'm quite thankful that my inner child keeps excitedly babbling on in my head. While some might say it's a distraction, I actually see him as my little voice of reason. There's a wisdom there that's so silly and simple that I can't help but follow along. My adult brain tends to overthink everything in a way that's mostly unproductive.

That's why you'll often find me writing stories about my childhood. Honoring that little boy is the least I could do for all of the inspiration he's provided me over the years. But, I fully realize that learning how to play again can be tougher than it seems. Now that we're all grown up, playing around and being silly can become a relic of the past. One should get serious about one's life at some point, right? We can't spend each day riding around on toy trains.

Well, I'm not advocating that one should ignore getting all of the important things done in life. I'm just stressing that it's worth stopping every so often to make sure the things we are doing are truly important. So many times, I find myself fretting over something that I later realize doesn't matter to anyone at all. And I can almost hear my inner child giggling back at me.

. . .

THE JOURNEY BEGINS

NEVER GROW UP. It's overrated and tedious. And keeping that spirit of your inner child alive and thriving will make growing old, which *is* terribly inevitable, a far more enjoyable experience. We were all born perfectly lovely, amazing, and limitless creative beings. When I hear someone say, "I'm not creative" I always want to jump in and correct them to say, "I'm not being creative *anymore*. I grew out of it." That's the reality, after all. But, no matter how many years go by, that little child who instinctively knew how to draw, play, create, and tell stories lives inside each of us, waiting for an invitation to fly.

I know that I can likely come across as a bit goofy at times. I'll get way too excited about a new animated movie coming out and see a toy online that I simply must obtain immediately. But, if that's the only side effect of letting my inner child take charge, then it's a harmless and joyous one indeed!

. . .

My only hope in sharing all of this is that I can inspire people to take a bit of time to pause and enjoy that little child inside. See the world through those eyes and watch it start to sparkle a bit. The following are collected musings and rambles written by me, with the help of that little boy inside. I don't have a method, approach, or lists of steps to share to help people rediscover their inner child. That would only bore that kid. No, instead, I'll just take you on a field trip through a world of thoughts, images and imagination. Bits of my life that you might recognize as it resembles bits of your own. I hope you'll laugh, have a happy cry, and smile on this trip. But, mostly, I just hope you and *your* inner child both enjoy the ride!

DAYS TO CELEBRATE

Once, I spent the entire month of November exploring the various National and World Days that happened each day of that month. I love these fun celebrations and they were ultimately what gave me the idea to found World Watercolor Month in July. So join me now for a little collection of stories I call, Days To Celebrate.

WORLD CLICHÉ DAY

Though there was a time when I wanted to be a writer, I realize I've always been at the end of the pecking order. I write like people talk and not in a lofty literary way, so as luck would have it, it's World Cliché Day! You could have knocked me over with a feather! I can do this with one hand tied behind my back and tongue firmly planted in cheek!

I doodlewashed a visual cliché to celebrate the day, as I've always wanted to sketch a stack of books, and putting an apple on top was just the icing on the cake. My brain was bursting with ideas for this one and I just couldn't sit still, but an idle mind is the devil's playground, so it's best to go for broke. After all, laughter *is* the best medicine.

It's not that I haven't tried to write with the best of them, it's just that, when push comes to shove, I don't want to sweat the details. Trying to clean up my writing is like putting lipstick on a pig. You could, but you'd just have a pig that's fit to be tied and you'd also likely be bored to tears. I love puns and will happily butcher the English language to get a point across, probably due to my years in marketing and advertising.

I don't have the patience to dot my i's and cross my t's, when I'm trying to tell a story. While spending a few years in big corporate America, I was assaulted with hundreds of buzzwords that made people sound dumb as a post. I used to get my kicks by inventing buzzwords and phrases to see how many people I could get to use them. Turns out, a lot! Just say something as serious as a heart attack, pretend you're eating your own dog food, and you'll have everyone chanting right along with you.

In case you're wondering, the difference between a cliché and a corporate buzzword is that a cliché actually makes some sense. Buzzwords simply prove the more we learn the less we know, and unless you are the lead dog, the view never changes. So you might as well jump on the bandwagon, or else risk being told that you zigged when you should have zagged.

In that environment, I stuck out like a sore thumb and always felt like I was swimming against the tide. The one salmon not swimming upstream. I understand that a house divided can't stand, but trying to pretend you *don't* see the absurdity in it all was too exhausting. If I'm going to sound dumb, I prefer to be dumb as a fox. But in that world you're damned if you do, and damned if you don't, so I'm happy as a clam to no longer be there.

Instead, these days, I've let bygones be bygones and you'll now find me always giving 110% to things I can actually care about. And though I love clichés, I know I've opened Pandora's box here and it's making me sound mad as a hatter. But we've lovingly built these little words and phrases as a culture and, now that they're out, you just can't put the toothpaste back in the tube. They are a part of who we are, and as beautiful as the day is long.

Clichés are as good as gold, albeit fool's gold, but still something to celebrate! And though sometimes in life you're the windshield and sometimes you're the bug, a good cliché will make everything right as rain again. How else would we learn that you can't swing a dead cat or take knickers off a bare arse? But if you don't feel you're quite a master of cliché yet, start slowly, as you must crawl before you can walk and, sometimes, you have to break a few eggs before you can make an omelette.

Okay, I should probably quit while I'm ahead and if you've made it this far you might be about to lose your mind. Only time will tell. But when you're at your next party, try to use as many clichés as possible to astound your friends. I've given you a head-start because, in this little essay, I've already implanted *over 50* of them in your brain! How's that for a topper? Someday, you will thank me for this.

WORLD TELEVISION DAY

November 21st is World Television Day, and this one is relatively official as it's sanctioned by the United Nations. It's not just a day to watch more TV, but a reminder of what television represents, which the UN says is a "symbol for communication and globalization in the contemporary world." Quite a mouthful, but there you have it.

Things have changed quite a bit as you don't even need a television anymore to catch your favorite shows, nor do you have to watch them at a specific time. But there was something magical about an era with appointment viewing, and having to wait for your favorite show each week. Back then, televisions had backs on them and required everyone in the family to pitch in just to move one across the room.

When I was a kid, the best television night was Saturday night because I got to stay up late with ABC's one-two punch of *Love Boat* followed by *Fantasy Island*. If I was super lucky, I even got to stay up to watch *Saturday Night Live*, which was always incredibly fun. But the real fun came on Sunday, when one of my favorite shows aired – *Murder, She Wrote*, starring the amazing Angela Lansbury.

I realize that this show was meant for women over 40, but how could anyone resist the spunky mystery author turned real-life detective, Jessica Fletcher, as she brilliantly solves a myriad of murders. Obviously, any sane person would have moved the hell out of Cabot Cove since the odds of getting murdered there were nearly 100%. But, at least you could rest easy knowing Jessica would skillfully put your killers in their rightful place after you're gone.

Jessica would travel frequently and people would also die wherever she was, so one had to wonder why she was ever invited to go anywhere. No matter where Jessica went, she was also recognized by everyone who saw her, which is amazing considering she only wrote books. Much of this was due to the fact that the odds of being related to Jessica Fletcher were also 100%. She had an endless list of relatives that she would always help, even though she never managed to have children of her own.

I was shocked to discover *Murder, She Wrote* was also one of Philippe's favorite shows. Apparently, we were both middle-aged women in a former life, which is equally comforting and disconcerting. Luckily, for a period of time, all of the seasons were on Netflix so we could binge watch whenever we liked and see our Jessica's face wildly smiling in freeze frame at the successful completion of each one.

Even if they were a bit ridiculous, what I liked about these older shows was that they were all attempting to tell you a story. Later, television would move to a million "reality" shows that successfully turned most of the nation into peeping Toms and sent talented writers to the unemployment lines. As for me, I'll always have a soft spot for shows with a plot.

So, today is the day to enjoy some of *your* favorite television shows and a time to remember those shows you used to love. Television is definitely one of the most influential inventions in history, so it's nice to see it gets to have its own special day to be celebrated.

NATIONAL APPLE CIDER DAY

Today is a time to kick back with a mug of apple cider and celebrate. In North America, this means the non-alcoholic beverage (unfiltered apple juice) versus the traditional kind, which is called hard cider. To the rest of the world, it's just the fermented concoction with anywhere from 1-12% alcohol content. So the choice is yours really.

I find it interesting that the type of apple best suited for cider and brandy is what's called a "spitter." This is a fruit so bitter and tannic that one's first instinct is to spit it out and frantically look for something sweet to lick. But ferment those bad boys and you've got yourself a wonderful beverage, with low alcohol, that was perfect for early world dwellers who wanted a refreshing drink without all of the cholera.

Now the good news about American apple cider is that it can be made into an array of alcoholic beverages, so you're not stuck with one kind. And, of course, you can also just drink it straight, without the alcohol, but then you should really start calling it by a more world-friendly name. Something more accurate like I used as a kid when I referred to it as "cloudy apple juice."

Cider is sort of doomed to be low in alcohol content because the apples themselves are so low in sugar. I'm not a big fan of cider as it sort of just tastes like a cheap version of a real drink. Like a sparkling wine with less sparkle and a strange apple-y aftertaste that wasn't supposed to be there. And in all honestly, at the end of the day, I think I'd rather just eat an apple and be done with it.

Beyond the "cloudy apple juice" I had as a child, my mom always had a hot spice tea mix during the colder months, which was a concoction of packets of other mixes, from Lipton, KoolAid, and Tang. The only ingredient not engineered in a laboratory was sugar, but adding it made one feel like they were more involved. Like "baking" with pre-made cookie dough… that's *also* been pre-sliced. Though perhaps this was even more ridiculous as this mix was something your cat, running across the kitchen counter, could have created entirely by accident.

But, for today, it's time to pour a glass of whatever you call cider and enjoy! These celebration days can be a bit ridiculous, so feel free to mold them and reinvent them into something that works for you. Or, if you're like me and have trouble following rules entirely, pour yourself a nice glass of wine and call it cider. Really, nobody is going to know.

AREA CODE DAY

On November 10th, we celebrate Area Code Day, which pays homage to a now bygone era where area codes actually mattered. The area code system was developed by AT&T and Bell Laboratories in the 1940's, and went into effect in 1947. It was called the North American Numbering Plan and included the United States and Canada.

Back when phones had rotary dials, lower numbers had shorter "dial pulls" and were therefore easier to call. This is why areas with high population often had lower numbers, like New York's famous 212 area code. Before mobile phones, moving to a new city meant changing your number and, well, your whole identity really, by adopting a new area code.

When I was a kid, we still had a rotary dial phone for a time and I thought they were fun. It felt like you were actually doing something magical in order to create a call. Of course if you messed up on the final bit of the number it was frustrating because you had to start all over or risk calling the entirely wrong person. Since I didn't like to actually talk to anyone on the phone, even back then, I would just dial short and wait for the amusingly horrible tones that signaled you'd just messed up.

The push button phones came and killed that magic. But they came with one of the greatest inventions at the time – the extra-long curly cord. It was all the rage to raid Radio Shack and get the absolute longest cord available so you could freely move throughout your house while talking on the phone. Long before smart phones, we were already trying to figure out how to do something, *anything* else, while talking to another person.

The extra-long curly cord was probably more dangerous than yard darts as it was often circling the furniture, tripping people on their way to the kitchen, and nearly strangling the family dog. If you wanted "privacy" for your important call, you'd simply pull the curly cord as far as you could and into the bathroom. There, you could finally take your call in peace, and, of course, do something else while talking to another person.

It was a huge deal when we finally got a cordless phone in the house. It looked like something from the Jetsons, and we were all excited to leave the horrors of the curly cord behind us. We quickly learned that without a cord, however, there's no reliable way to keep track of the phone and it would often be lost behind couch cushions or left sitting on the bathroom sink. But, it was *so* cool.

Soon after college, I got my first mobile phone. These were less impressive. They were the size of a regular handset, which made you look like a crazy person who had wandered into the street with your cordless phone. If you were not of the persuasion to carry a purse, then figuring out what the hell to do with it in transit was particularly worrisome. So I just left mine in the car and used it only for emergencies, which is still the only way I tend to make personal phone calls.

But as mobile phones evolved into smart phones, long distance calls became a thing of the past, and people could keep their number even when they moved. The poor area code has lost its ability to geolocate us. While those who remember these times still throw parties when securing a coveted New York 212, the next generation just shrugs, says a name into their earbuds and starts talking to someone. They didn't have to memorize the number that they're calling, and couldn't tell you any of the digits, much less the area code.

For some of us, though, we can celebrate Area Code Day with memories of how life once was. Back in the days of the curly cord, when telling someone your area code was as revealing as telling them where you went to college. Three amazing little numbers that changed the world as we knew it. Little numbers that we never suspected could lose their magic, until the world would change once again.

ABSURDITY DAY

Today is a day to sit back and recall the many absurd things that have happened in our lives or things that are still happening each day. It's also a day to actually add to this list by doing something completely ridiculous and random that you've always wanted to try. For example, I have been harboring a strange desire to doodlewash a flying pig, so this was a good day for that.

Sometimes, it's rather difficult to determine what's actually absurd. It really depends on who you are and where you are. I've mentioned before Philippe's shock at discovering some of America's habits, but these aren't considered absurd, just part of living in this country. So if you're American, and stumped on how to celebrate this one, it's equally likely that to someone in *another* country, you're already doing it.

When Philippe was first visiting from Paris, I took him out to dinner at a local Mexican restaurant. I thought it would be fine as it was actual Mexican food, not the Tex-Mex version which is really just a game of "food hide-and-seek" in a pool of orange cheese. Unfortunately, the restaurant had decided to serve it with American-sized portions and Philippe ate the entire thing out of habit. The remainder of the evening was spent with him clutching his stomach in pain and taking short breaths as though he were about to deliver our first child.

Beyond the absurdity of portion size in American meals, there's often the complete lack of vegetables or any meaningful fiber. This always leads Philippe to ask, "How do Americans poop?" It never occurred to me anymore, since I mostly eat vegetables now, but this was a very good question. I watch people out eating, as every green thing on a plate is pushed to the side and treated as garnish, and have to wonder the very same thing.

When we first went out driving here, Philippe would ask about all of the American flags. I'm so used to seeing them that I've totally blocked them out. But, he was confused as to why people had them *everywhere*. "I don't understand," he said, "yeah, we're in America, we get it!" as a too big to be driven in the city truck burped past us with flags flapping on each side. "They're just proud of this country," I said as a man wearing a coat that looked like a flag walked by. And that's when I realized it was actually absurd.

Everything from weather to cooking was made needlessly complex for Philippe because America is one of the only countries in the world *not* using the metric system (the only other two are Burma and Liberia). "It says a heaping cup," Philippe remarked while cooking, "what the hell is a cup? Which cup? Heaping?" I pointed him to the measuring cups and he said, "C'est pas vrai! That's so stupid and imprecise! Why don't they just measure in handfuls or fingernails?" The next day, we bought a scale that measured in grams.

But, the absurdity didn't stop in the kitchen, of course. I was questioned as to "whose feet" one uses to determine distance. This is a bit embarrassing as feet and pounds are things that were necessary in the old days when people didn't know any better, much like the Electoral College. To still be using these antiquated systems today, just makes us seem, well… rather absurd (though Fahrenheit is *still* twice as precise as Celsius when setting your air conditioning so there's a tiny something we got right!).

America is already an absurd place, so maybe that's why so many people like it. We're not weighed down with horrible logic. We just live happily inside our absurdity bubble assuming everyone else must be wrong. So today, add a heaping cup of absurdity to whatever it is *you* plan to do and have a ridiculously good time!

CABINET OF CURIOSITIES

When I first started sketching and blogging, I devoted an entire month to collecting bits of things that I referred to as my *cabinet of curiosities*. For those of you who don't know what this particular type of cabinet is, according to author Patrick Mauriès, they were "rooms of wonders... the astonishing creation of collectors who wished to gather together everything, all knowledge – animal, vegetable, or man-made – into a single unimaginable space. An entire universe in miniature."

Cool, huh? The unimaginable space, in my case, was simply a new miniature sketchbook I'd purchased recently. So, join me now for a little collection of stories those tiny sketches inspired.

MAGIC LANTERN

I've always been fascinated with vintage cameras and other image-producing objects. This tiny sketch is of something called a magic lantern or laterna magica. It was an early type of image projector that used pictures on sheets of glass, and either sunlight, candles or oil lamps to project light. It was developed in the 17th century and commonly used for educational and entertainment purposes.

Today, it sits downstairs in a box as I managed to acquire one on eBay a few years back. I was so excited that I neglected to realize the obvious. That nobody needs a magic lantern in the 21st century, and this was a ridiculous waste of money. But it looked so cool! Modern objects just don't have the class and attention to detail, choosing cheap over charming most of the time.

When I was in grade school, I was deemed to be rather smart and therefore enrolled in an independent study course. What this meant was that, twice a year, I could choose any subject I wanted to explore in more depth and detail. One of my independent study subjects was animation, and I was so excited to get started.

I first tried drawing on individual film cells with a marker, but quickly lost interest. After about 5 cells, I had only managed to produce a stick figure that appeared to be squatting to relief himself. This was not satisfying and simply wouldn't do for my directorial debut, so I immediately began looking for other options.

I discovered that the school actually had a video camera, and the notion of doing a stop-motion animation was born. This was many, many years ago, so the camera was the size of a small suitcase and weighed more than I did at the time. I wasn't daunted because every stop-motion director worth a grain of salt knew that a tripod was required for absolute precision.

My main character was an egg-shaped ball of white fur, appropriately named Fluffy, and he had just two large googly eyes, dowel rods for legs and light blue shoes "borrowed" from Mr. Potato Head. It was just as I was beginning my epic shoot that I realized the script also required arms. So, a couple of pipe cleaners were jammed into the side seams.

Fluffy's story was a bit weird because, in my enthusiasm, I pre-made all of the props out of the first cool thing I saw. In this case, a stack of notecards shaped like various musical instruments. So, we began the story in a music shop, obviously, and Fluffy went around trying out each of the instruments. Perhaps it was his last-minute pipe cleaner arms or his googly-eyed lack of depth perception, but he systematically breaks each instrument he attempts to play.

After fleeing the shop, we hear a foreboding voice-over from a police radio, calling in the crime to dispatch. Okay… so I played the part of the police officer and my voice was anything but foreboding then, or even now for that matter. But you get the point. It was bad. Real bad for Fluffy.

As sirens wailed, Fluffy did the only thing he could think to do. Rush *back* into the scene of the crime and attempt to repair all of the destroyed instruments. Through the magic of stop motion, he was able to put everything back like he found it and escape before the authorities arrived. I was *then* asked to play this masterpiece of cinema for each of the other classes during a day-long premier in the library. Apparently, teaching kids that vandalism is okay, as long as you get away with it, was a lesson worth skipping regular class for.

Although I would end up working on a movie later in life, I never fully realized my childhood dreams. Perhaps, that's why I bought an expensive antique magic lantern. It reminds me of a time when I used to dream big and was never daunted by the idea that I couldn't do something. It's funny how as adults we always question ourselves and yet, as kids, we always assumed anything was possible. Sometimes, I wish I could go back to that time. A time when a white ball of fur named Fluffy could be the next big movie star, and I actually *believed* in magic.

CALLING MOM

My dad liked to collect things... well... sort of acquire things he suddenly took a fancy to. This old telephone was one of those things and it ended up following me around from house to house for many years before finally disappearing. I always liked this old phone (it looked like it had a face!), but never had a place to display it, nor knew how to hang it properly.

So, it just sat on the floor laying against various walls in various apartments and houses. This doodlewash is an ode to that old phone. And, since I now rarely use the "phone app" on my smartphone, preferring to text, this always reminds me of nearly the only person I talk to on the telephone – my mother.

My mother lives in Texas now and we only see each other a couple of times a year. Neither of us are particularly good about using a telephone, so it's not uncommon to go weeks without talking to each other. Our running joke is that whoever finally decides to break the silence and actually *call*, says, "Hi, it's me. I'm returning your call."

Not sure why I wouldn't call more because conversations with my mother are always entertaining, since I'm never sure what will pop out of her mouth. You're likely to hear bits of wisdom like these: "It's kind of like a porno… people say there's a story to it, but there's no story to it," or, "I'm kinda glad I grew up in the 50's. We didn't have to wear slingshots for underwear in the 50's," or "Well, *apparently*, having sex with a dead woman is only a misdemeanor."

I remember when I was talking to her about first meeting Philippe. I was excited to be traveling to Paris to spend time with him for a few weeks, but worried that my ability to speak Spanish was not going to be very helpful there. I was visiting my mother for Christmas and had just ordered a new in-depth French language course. This was the conversation:

ME: So I'm trying to learn some French before I visit Philippe in Paris.
MOM: That's good! Have you seen those commercials for Rosetta Stone?
ME: No, I don't have cable, why?
MOM: There's this one with a 30 year old man on there and he says, "Now I can speak to my parents in Japanese!" I was like… if your parents wanted you to speak to them in Japanese, why the hell didn't they teach you?!"

This is the wonderful logic I grew up with, and, I have to admit, it's served me well in life. I really love hearing about the world as translated through my mother's eyes and ears. You usually feel like you're starting in the middle of the story, but that's all part of the fun. The conversation will take a whiplash turn from a political tirade to the inexplicable discovery that "their neighbor's cows were coming over and licking the siding on the house. I mean, what's *wrong* with those cows?!"

Everyone has a different relationship with their families as well as with their phones, but I'm just fine with mine. Sometimes it's the things you do the least that you remember the most. And out of all of the crazy things I've done in life, the most cherished memories will always be the simpler ones. Those rare and wonderful times when I remembered to press the phone app, and found myself calling mom.

SWATCH

This is a doodlewash of my watch because I wasn't sure what to sketch, and, while looking at the time, I was suddenly inspired. I guess someday I'll have drawn just about anything you can imagine and will seek more interesting subjects, but today, I'm still quite easily amused.

Philippe gave me this watch as a present on our first Christmas together. When we were in Paris earlier in that year, I was eyeing a watch like this while we were passing a Swatch store. I had never really thought about owning a watch by this brand as I didn't think they made anything that wasn't the color of fruit.

Later that year, I was thrilled when I received one from Philippe! It had exposed clockwork, which has always fascinated me. I'm not sure why, but the idea of that many tiny gears coming together to make something function amazes me. And it had the perfect band, as I can only wear fabric or leather because my wrists are roughly the size of an eight year old girl's.

And, not only does it have clockwork showing, it actually *is* a completely mechanical watch, powered only by movement. On me, this means it always runs about five minutes fast. Also, each month you have to reset it in order to get the date to display properly. I'm too lazy to bother with this. So, when anyone asks me the date on the street, they walk away roughly three days earlier.

When I received this watch, for all I knew, this was going to be my only reminder of my time with Philippe. We were always running out of time back then. Being together was like looking at the ocean for the last time on a beach you've visited for the first time. You make a silent wish that you'll be back. But, in the end, you just never know for sure if that wish will come true.

Today, with all of the hours and minutes ticking away, it never feels like I can get everything done. But whenever I feel like I'm not accomplishing the things that I want fast enough, I just look at this little reminder on my wrist and stop worrying. Things always work out, and there's no need to rush. I've got time.

BLUE YELLOW MACAW

This is a blue and yellow macaw. I primarily chose him because I noticed I was drawing too many brown things lately. Also, I've always loved parrots. There's something sort of awesome about an animal that can mimic human speech, and the blue and yellow macaw is one of the better talkers. Of course, if you share a home with one, you would really need to be careful what you say as they're not good at keeping secrets.

I've always loved animals, and particularly birds. And, I once wanted to become a bird watcher. This wasn't a constant passion, but something I became suddenly passionate about as a kid when I stumbled across a copy of Audubon Magazine. I was shocked that more people my age hadn't thought to become a "birder" as it seemed like exciting and interesting work. It wasn't long before I realized the sheer amount of sitting and waiting involved, which was also the reason why most of my peers were over the age of 60.

After sitting and staring at a tree for 30 minutes, waiting for something to appear so I could identify it, I got bored and started carving a bird out of a stick instead. I'd just gotten one of those Swiss Army pocket knives and wanted to test it out. It was classic red and, beyond its nice selection of knives and a pair of scissors, there was even a spoon and fork! (For those occasions when you are stranded and without food, but take comfort in knowing you *could* eat it properly if you weren't about to starve to death).

My wooden stick bird was a disaster and looked more like a beaked snake that hadn't finished shedding its skin. Just 45 minutes into this silly adventure, I was ready to crawl out of mine. My dreams of birding had been crushed again by the deathly club of my attention deficit problems (kids weren't medicated to be "made normal" back then, so I was left alone to grow up "naturally unique").

With apparently no ability to actually find an interesting bird, much less carve it out of a stick, I was at a loss for how to start this new hobby. At the time, I didn't realize that birding was something that also involved travel in order to experience more variety. I had just assumed that since birds could fly anywhere, once they knew I was watching for them, they would just fly over and say hello. No bird ever did. Not even a parrot, and they could have actually *said* it.

So today, I'll happily merge my lost long, day long hobby with my new one and do a little birding whenever I can on doodlewash.com. With just a little bit of ink and some paint, I can make *any* bird I like appear now! It may not get me honored by the Audubon Society as the world's next great "bird nerd" but it will let me fulfill my childhood dreams of finally coming face to face with a bright blue and yellow macaw.

NEIGHBORHOOD CAT

I decided to doodlewash a cat for the first time today, since I think I still have Halloween on the brain and they are always a star player. I was going to try a black one, but opted for a gray tabby I've seen around the neighborhood instead. I wasn't sure how to handle all of the hair and whiskers, so I just whisked some white gouache on it at the the end.

Growing up, and all through adulthood, I've only ever had dogs. It wasn't until I was grown that I realized I had a mild allergy to cats, so this worked out well. I think cats are beautiful, but prefer the ones that are social and act more like dogs. The aloof cats confound me as they seem more like a pet "prop" rather than actual companions. The tabby sketched here roams the neighborhood and, I've never seen where it lives. And, I'm only assuming it has a home because it's hard to tell with cats sometimes.

I remember visiting a couple, a few years back, and

when I sat down and they handed me a drink, their cat jumped up on my lap. I screamed loudly. Not because the appearance was so sudden, but because this particular cat was completely hairless and ancient. They just smiled and said, "That's our little baby" and I tried desperately to pass it off as simply a case of being startled, while trying very hard to remove the look of disgust and horror from my face.

I learned that this cat was over 26 years old and that the lack of hair was on purpose. Apparently, it was a Sphinx and they had been giving it better care than given to most children. But seeing a bald cat for the first time is still a little disconcerting and takes some getting used to. As it turns out, even without the hair, these cats are *not* hypoallergenic so it was a relatively short evening.

On a visit to another cat house (oh wait… house with cats in it, not the other kind), I was shocked once again to find this couple had trained their cat to use the toilet. Admittedly, this sounds awesome, as the smell of kitty litter in a house can usually be detected from the driveway by people like me who don't live with cats daily. But when you walk in on a cat doing his business on the toilet you were hoping to use, it's more than a little disturbing. Admittedly, I should have knocked, but they really should have thought to train Whiskers to lock the door behind him first.

I finally met my first dog-like cat soon after that, and I was immediately in love. The cat was a yellow tabby and so ridiculously cute that you immediately wanted to cuddle up next to it. And that's exactly what it wanted to do, so allergies be damned I did. And, it was totally worth the itching and sneezing. This cat was my new best friend for the night.

Though I don't think I'll ever own a cat as I still prefer dogs and dislike sneezing, I find them fascinating creatures. There's sort of an ancient wisdom in their eyes and secrets they will probably never reveal to us. And that makes them pretty cool. There's such a range of types and personalities with cats that I'm sure there's always a cat for any non-allergic person to enjoy. Even if they prefer to use your toilet over a litter box or are made entirely out of skin. Which admittedly… still sort of creeps me out.

CHILDHOOD FAVORITES

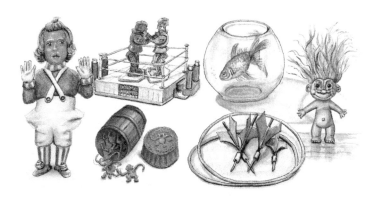

I felt like sharing some of my favorite bits of childhood with you. Those little things that made me smile when I was a much shorter person. I grew up during a time when the world was changing a bit more slowly, and every new thing was so fascinating. Today, we're not quite as easily impressed by new things. We tend to shrug and ask, "yeah… what else can it do?"

But back then, nearly every new thing felt like an innovation and a wonder to behold. So join me now as we head back to those days when everything was fascinating and awesome. Though much has changed in life since those days, it's difficult to avoid smiling when thinking back to those childhood favorites.

OOMPA-LOOMPAS

Just a few months after yours truly entered the world for the first time, these little things burst onto the cinema screen in *Willy Wonka & the Chocolate Factory*. It was a few years later, of course, before I finally got to see it, but I always thought it was super cool that the main little boy in the movie shared my name. It was the Oompa-Loompas that I remembered most from the movie because of just how bizarre they were. I have no idea why they popped into my head or why I thought to doodlewash one, but that's where we landed.

Basically, for anyone who's unfamiliar with the story, five lucky kids get to enter an elusive and eccentric chocolate maker's factory having procured golden tickets. Each time one misbehaves, they are met with some unfortunate fate and the Oompa-Loompas come to remove them from the scene while singing ominous moralizing songs about their misdeeds. They were knee-high, and they were orange, and they were absolutely terrifying. I remember thinking if I didn't complete my homework they might show up, popping their heads in my window, and start singing their insidiously catchy songs.

The movie was based on a book by Roald Dahl who is my all-time favorite author of children's books. His stories were super dark, didn't talk down to kids, and I loved them for that. His original Oompa-Loompas (called Whipple-Scrumpets before publication) started out as African pygmies until he rewrote them to be white-skinned and blonde. The movie version opted for a more colorful version with orange skin and green hair. In the book, there were whole families of Oompa-Loompas with the men wearing skins, women wearing leaves, and children simply running around naked. This was, thankfully, also changed for the movie version.

The movie was creepy, but also one of my favorites as a kid. Willy Wonka, played by Gene Wilder, was a fascinatingly odd and wonderfully crazy character (as played by Johnny Depp years later, he was just a creepy pervert). The original movie contained a song called "Cheer Up Charlie" and this soon became something my family members would repeat to me, much to my dismay, whenever I got grumpy. Slightly better than having the other kids at school constantly say, "Sorry Charlie" thanks to those darn Starkist Tuna commercials.

But I loved the book much more than the movie. In fact, I preferred books to movies when I was a kid. Still do actually. There's just something more fun about being able to imagine something for myself rather than having someone else show me exactly what they think it should look like. Now, it's really hard to get this version of an Oompa-Loompa out of my brain. These orange little guys have been burned into my head since childhood, thanks to that small screen in my living room. Perhaps that's why Roald Dahl had his Oompa-Loompas make this plea to kids everywhere…

"Oh, books, what books they used to know,
   Those children living long ago!
   So please, oh please, we beg, we pray, go throw your TV set away,
   And in its place you can install,
   A lovely bookshelf on the wall."
   ~*Roald Dahl, Charlie And The Chocolate Factory, 1964*

LAWN DARTS

A trip down memory lane wouldn't be complete for me if I didn't mention a favorite backyard game called Lawn Darts. This terrifying game consisted of sharp, weighted metal stakes with colorful fins, like a hideously enlarged dart you might find in a neighborhood bar. Large for a dart, but still a rather compact little game that could be easily taken from house to house. These little "fun for the whole family" missiles were stupidly dangerous, and attempts to ban them in the 70's failed, not succeeding until 1988. So, of course, my family kept playing with them assuming they must be safe.

I remember my older cousins used to play this game and when I got older myself, I tried it as well. The goal was pretty simple as you just had to get your dart to impale the grass inside the little yellow hula hoop. Thankfully, everyone would usually hide on one side while flinging the little missiles across the yard, and, at least for my family, there were never any casualties. But that didn't mean it was actually safe so much as we were just rather lucky. If someone had marketed a family game called "Be A Circus Knife Thrower" heads might have turned, but these little weapons managed to sail the skies for decades.

Being a little child in the 70's was actually quite easy as there were absolutely no rules. No helmets to wear if you wanted to ride your bike somewhere and no seat belts to bother with when riding in a car (it wasn't even required to put seat belts *in* a car until the late 60's). Looking back, it seems astonishing that any of us survived, but I guess now there are worse things to be afraid of, so maybe it's not so different after all.

Although I miss some things from childhood that were removed out of fear, I highly support the fear of lawn darts. These things were just scary. But, even so, the memories of my family gathering together at my aunt's house are wonderful. Playing lawn darts meant we were just killing time until dessert was served, which was my favorite part of the day. Though a less lethal game would have been appreciated, we at least came together often to enjoy a little family fun. That's something we stopped doing as we all got older and that's *really* the thing I miss most.

ROCK 'EM SOCK 'EM ROBOTS

Here we have a doodlewash of a little fighting game featuring robots that I loved when I was a kid. Of course, if you were a kid in the U.K. at the time, your game didn't mention the cool robots and was weirdly renamed to Raving Bonkers. Sorry about that. But here in the U.S., it was all about the red and blue robots who, through no particular backstory, were dead set on kicking each other's ass.

Each player takes control of a bot: the "Red Rocker" or the "Blue Bomber" who are waiting in a bright yellow boxing ring (If you were a kid in the 80's who liked Transformers, you might have had the Megatron and Optimus version). By pushing plunger buttons on a pair of joysticks, players try to punch the other robot's lights out. If you smack the other robot just right under the chin, its head pops up and you win the round. That was it, actually, which sounds a little dull when you write about it, but it was super fun to play!

There's just something about controlling a physical robot that is so much cooler than a video game. Admittedly, it played like an elaborate game of thumb wrestling and didn't stay exciting for very long during a given session. But in those spurts of time when we pulled out the game and played a few rounds, it was very engaging. Unlike video games, there were no bullets and no bloodshed. Just a robot who malfunctions briefly until you jam his head back down into place.

I wasn't one of those rough and tumble boys. I never liked sports of any kind and I preferred a good book or playing the piano instead. But this was a "sport" even I could enjoy and participate in, without feeling like a completely out-of-place idiot. It was perfect! So, I have a love for these little guys for providing a little rough sport to my over-cultured, nerdy childhood. If you're curious, I was always "Red Rocker." But, to this day, I have absolutely no idea why.

FISH IN A BOWL

I was always fascinated with goldfish as a kid. They seemed like they were trying to communicate (most likely saying, "get me the hell out of this tiny bowl you jerk!") and always seemed incredibly bored. Lots of my friends had them when I was growing up because they were the go-to low maintenance pet. All of them had asked for a hamster, dog or cat and were instead "surprised" with one of these instead and told not to touch it.

Since I was one of the kids lucky enough to be given a hamster, I wasn't allowed to also have a goldfish. When my whining grew too great, my mother finally gave in and got me my very own consolation prize: Sea-Monkeys. Instead of being disappointed, I was absolutely thrilled and thought I had really scored something magical. That was until I discovered they were *not* actual little monkeys who lived in water, but something else entirely.

The packaging showed a disturbingly naked family of human-like creatures with tails who were wearing crowns. Along with this was the exciting proclamation that these were "*Live* Sea-Monkeys," which was good as nobody ever wants to receive a dead pet. I vaguely remembered the ads from my comic books and so I was intrigued. After all, they had promised these were "a bowl full of happiness you can grow yourself" and, best of all, they are "so eager to please – they can even be 'trained'!" The fact that "trained" was in quotes had escaped me entirely during my initial excitement.

Unfortunately, once the "live eggs" hatched, what appeared was something that looked like floating pieces of lint. I used the growth food as instructed, however, they never grew up to become that happy family from the box and remained seemingly lifeless microscopic sea creatures. Refusing to give up, I attempted to "train" them as described and play some music to watch them dance. They just stopped moving entirely. This was when I realized it was a hoax. I mean honestly, who could resist the sultry belting of Tina Turner or not bounce around happily when hearing the theme from Footloose?

Once, as an adult, I almost bought some Sea-Monkeys just to see if maybe things had changed. But I resisted. I didn't want to live through the disappointment again should the same outcome occur. And if they *had* grown up to become the happy family on the package, I would have just felt bad that they had to live in a tiny bowl and likely found their nudist lifestyle to be uncomfortably awkward. So, I think I'll just stick with dogs. Now that I'm old enough to have one without having to ask my parents first.

BARREL OF MONKEYS

One of the most memorable little things from my childhood is also the simplest. It was a tiny red plastic barrel filled with little plastic monkeys that my grandmother kept on a bookshelf. These were super inexpensive and available just about everywhere by the 70's, but I only remember playing when I went to visit my grandmother's farm. Looking back, I doubt she even purchased it herself as I'm sure it was just something brought by a cousin one Christmas and forgotten. But in my mind, it always takes me back to her.

The phrase "more fun than a barrel of monkeys" had been around for years before anyone decided to riff on it and make it into a game. Actually the very first phrase was "box of monkeys" since that's how they were transported to America. This shifted immediately to include "barrel" as those were used for alcohol so the connotation was doubly fun! (Also, there was a saying called "sucking the monkey" which meant drinking alcohol straight from the barrel, not, thankfully, what immediately comes to mind when you first read that phrase.)

Barrel of Monkeys consisted of grabbing one little monkey and then using it to pick up the other monkeys, forming a monkey chain. The longer the chain got, the more difficult it became to hook another monkey and if you dropped one your turn was over. Yep… that's the whole game. But it was still pretty addictive.

According to Wikipedia, a Dr. Gilbert Patterson holds the record for making the fastest chain, but a Sir Robert Donald of Orange County has the unofficial fastest claim (as well as two first names and the dubious honor of being knighted in California). Donald's recorded game is allegedly being sent in for review to the unsubstantiated "North American Barrel of Monkeys Association" which proves one mustn't always take Wikipedia terribly seriously.

But for me, this little game will always bring back memories of hanging out on my grandmother's farm. There you would find me, sitting in a small chair by the window, having just eaten my Corn Flakes for supper while reading all of the cartoons in her copies of *Reader's Digest*. Not quite satisfied with the evening's entertainment, I would always reach for that little red plastic barrel. This was many years ago now, during that wonderful, simpler time, when there was really nothing more fun than a barrel of monkeys.

TROLL DOLLS

Here's a little thing that started as a fad in the 60's, then made flash comebacks each decade after that. The first troll doll was created in 1959 when a Danish fisherman and woodcutter named Thomas Dam. He couldn't afford a Christmas gift for his young daughter Lila, so he carved a doll from his imagination. When other kids in town wanted them too, the company "Dam Things" was formed and the rest, as they say, is history.

When I was a kid, these things were often one of the prizes at amusement parks, could be fished out of the arcade's skill crane game, or purchased as a pencil topper. The last version was the most fun, not only for the miniature size, but because you could smooth the hair up to a point and then spin the pencil between your palms as fast as you could to create the worst hair day ever for the hideously cute little thing. For some reason that escapes me now, this was perfectly hilarious and never got old.

I don't think I'd ever requested a troll doll, but the "Dam Things" were so prevalent that it was nearly impossible not to end up with a tiny one at some point. They weren't always naked and genderless, as they also came in various outfits or people made different outfits for them. But I didn't like the ones with outfits as they felt like dolls to me, and the naked ones just felt like toys. A distinction that only a psychiatrist could explain properly.

But never fear, if you missed out on these guys, Dreamworks bought the license and brought Trolls back to life in movie form. Again, something you may have never asked for, but apparently that's just how these trolls work. They sort of force their way into your life like that. Unlike Smurfs, though, these guys were always just inanimate objects for me and that was part of the charm I think. If one started talking, I might feel weird jabbing a pencil up its butt and spinning it 'til its hair explodes! That would just spoil all of the fun.

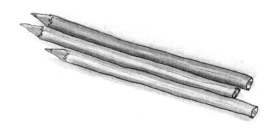

WHEN THE MUSIC PLAYS

The following collection is about another art form that is near and dear to my heart. Music. Music has an incredible way of stirring emotion and bringing back all sorts of memories. These are some of mine, that I hope, in the end, will also inspire lovely memories of your own. So join me now as we embark on a musical journey together and experience some of those wonderful stories that happen, when the music plays.

MY FAVORITE SONG

Choosing a single favorite song is an impossible task to be sure. So much depends on your mood and the particular time period that you're living through at the moment. I jumped back to the 70's for this doodlewash and depicted the origin of my love of music itself. Cassette tapes were still considered experimental and the sound quality had just caught up with 8-track tapes. Those were the large cumbersome things that my dad was quite proud to have in his car when I was little.

When we got a new car with a cassette player, my mother asked me what I thought of it and I told her that I hated it. She asked me why, and I simply said, "No Ray Charles." His soulful melodies, in my little mind, only came on that giant 8-track and the second I spied that new *tiny* slot in the dashboard, I knew that things had changed for the worse. But thankfully, we still had records that I could listen to and that was a lovely thing indeed. The record players were often made with handles as though they were actually portable, when in reality they never really left the room they were first plunked down in. They weighed a ton so it was easier to just enjoy the music wherever it landed.

When you're a little kid, you don't usually get to choose the music that gets played in the house, so you adapt to the tastes of your parents. In my case, and in the case of the early 70's in general, folk music and singer-songwriter hits were still all the rage. I used to love listening to their beloved 60's music as Peter, Paul and Mary sang Puff The Magic Dragon, although it would be years before I understood what the song actually meant. Beyond just listening to songs, I loved to sing along with them. I've no idea if I was any good back then, but years later, I would actually sing professionally for a brief period, so the early practice must have helped.

Songs had a way of speaking directly to my heart and, over the years, there would be new favorite songs depending on my mood. When I reached high school, the cassette tape had taken over completely and the fact that you could record your own tracks onto one was amazing. Getting a "mix tape" from a friend, or even better, a love interest, was the most incredible thing in the world. It was like getting a love note of recorded poetry, even though the songs were all written by other people. It was the choices of the tracks themselves that made it special.

Fast forward to now, and it's not surprising that watercolor holds the same affection for me. Its unruly yet rhythmic movements express surprising emotions that still seem inevitable once they appear. Like the turning point of any great story. I don't sing much anymore, save those odd times when I find myself driving alone in the car and hoping the people around me think there's actually music playing. But, each day, I sit down for a brief little moment and enjoy the melody of watercolor. I've literally no clue what I'll choose to paint, and even less clue as to what will appear on the paper or what words I might write that day. This, for me, is why it's so much fun!

I've never been a fan of knowing exactly what would happen next. I prefer to live life with a healthy appetite for surprise. Sure, I have a thousand dreams, but I know that I can't actually *force* them to happen. I can, instead, make space in my life for the art of the possible to occur. Good things will always happen, when the time is right. Until then, I just keep moving forward and enjoying the moments that come my way. Each one, no matter how simple, becomes another note in the melody of life. In those beautiful moments, when they occur, I can say without a doubt, that it's my favorite song.

PLAYING THE VIOLIN

Back when I was in grade school, my first introduction to harmony came by playing my very first instrument, which was a violin. I was in 4th grade at the time and chose the violin mainly because I didn't want to wait a year before they'd let me play a wind instrument. I'm not sure why this was the case, but playing a stringed instrument like this is rather difficult, and perhaps they wanted us to get a head start. The downside to this, of course, is that parents had to endure noises that sounded less like music and more like stretching a cat in half.

Early sounds on the violin are harsh and loathsome noises. What eventually turns into something akin to music, with a bit more practice, first begins with raking a horse hair bow across strings making horrible squeaks and shrill squawks. When all of us would come together and play in those first years, it was anything but harmonious. We received applause and accolades from teachers and parents after the performance, but I still remember looking out and seeing everyone wincing as though suffering from severe stomach pain.

Bless them for their lies, as I was perfectly willing to see myself as amazing and continued to practice and play throughout high school. Eventually, the squawks turned into something more lovely, and I was finally making music. I played in the high school orchestra and it was a thrill to hear all of those sounds from various instruments come together to create the most intricate and beautiful harmonies.

I never practiced as much as I should have back then, but still managed. There were other things catching my interest by that time, so I would just steal a few minutes each day to play a bit. Though others around me were far better, each and every day, I still improved. I challenged my way to one of the front chairs in my final year, just before our group got to play at Carnegie Hall in New York. It was a triumphant experience to play on that historic stage and I still remember the sound as it echoed and reverberated in scientific precision.

After high school, I put down the violin, and only managed to pick it up a couple more times a year later. It was eventually sold to get some extra money so I could continue to struggle through college. I'm not sure if I would have continued to play had I been one of the richer kids, but I was sad to see it disappear from my life. Sometimes, choices are simply made for us. Once I had enough money to afford another violin, I'd already moved on to other dreams and schemes.

Each time I see one, though, I'm taken back to those moments and I can still hear those vibrating harmonics like it was yesterday. Music that will always be trapped in my memories and soul. That's the wonderful thing about creating music and art. Years later, no matter which way our life chooses to turn, the urge will always be there. Whether it's longing to paint again, or remembering back to a wonderful time long gone when I was enthralled with musical dreams while happily playing the violin.

THAT TIME I PLAYED GUITAR

There was a time, way back when, that I played guitar for a very brief period. As a child of the 70's, I was in love with the singer-songwriters of the time. Amazingly talented people who could simply grab a guitar and write something catchy and incredible that moved my heart. Though I always wanted to play the guitar like they did, this wasn't an instrument taught in my school, so I ended up playing the violin instead. Don't get me wrong, I loved it, but a part of me still longed to strum a guitar and write songs. You can't really sing along while playing a violin.

It wasn't until high school that the urge grew too much for me, and I decided to try guitar. My dad bought me a mail order one which was delivered when we weren't home and the postman strangely thought the best place to conceal it was under the car in the driveway. Luckily, we found it before someone backed over it, and I soon began lessons. It was all a dream come true, until, months later, a car accident would change everything.

My guitar instructor was wonderful and introduced me to classical guitar music. This meant strumming with all fingers rather than using a guitar pick. I adored it and practiced like crazy, quickly becoming rather good, strumming my way through all kinds of wonderful music. Soon after, I began my last year of high school, excited to serenade my friends. But by the time the holiday season arrived, I was equally busy with lots of various holiday parties. I was President or Vice-President of several clubs and the end of the year meant hopping to various gatherings. It was driving home from the very last gathering, perhaps overly exhausted, that everything changed.

I don't quite remember what happened, but think I may have nodded off for a moment. Suddenly, there was a horrible sound of crushing metal and a fierce impact. I stumbled out of my crumpled car, still wearing a silly Christmas tie that played music. I don't have many memories of what happened next. The clearest memory after that was waking up in a hospital bed with two fractured hips. And, also, a faint feeling of thinking how creepy it must have been for whoever found me to see a stumbling boy mumbling "help me" to a slow, tinny, electronic rendition of Jingle Bells.

My head was bandaged when I awoke. My car had been partially severed in the crash as well. It was restored, without any visible scarring, though I still like to think of it as my Van Gogh moment. Soon, a giant bag of letters and cards arrived. Apparently, news travels fast and when it travels through the grapevine, people often get things wrong. Many thought I was dead, but I still appreciated their kind thoughts and well wishes. Not many people have a chance to hear what someone might say about them after they are gone.

But other than hobbling around on crutches for a few weeks, I was miraculously alive. One injury, however, was small yet devastating. The index finger of my right hand, was broken in several places. It healed only to a point, and with limited moment. I could still hold a violin bow, but I now lacked the coordination required to strum my beloved guitar. I was crushed and lost, at first, but soon discovered that I could still hold a pencil to write and draw. Especially easily, as it turns out, since my finger seemed to be slightly locked in that position. Life doesn't always work out like we hope, but if we continue to *have* hope, it always delivers something wonderful. And though I never became that singer-songwriter of my dreams, I don't have any regrets. Just a fond and lasting memory of that time I played guitar.

BEARS, PEARS, AND DIRTY DANCING

When Philippe and I were in Trader Joe's around the holidays one year, I saw that they had Harry & David pears. I used to love these at this time of year, but the store we had here closed, and I don't like the lack of immediate gratification that comes with ordering fruit online. He balked at the price, which was more than twice as much as a full bag and had only five pears. I insisted they were worth it, but after trying them, he only resigned to say they were "better, but not *that* much better to justify the cost." They were *totally* worth it!

Last night was the first show in our Broadway Across America season. We like getting season tickets because we end up seeing shows we'd never go see otherwise. This show was no exception as it was Dirty Dancing... yep... the movie... only *live*. Or, as the program proclaimed, the "Classic Story On Stage." But, as I overheard the woman behind me say during the performance as she shifted uncomfortably in her seat, "Ugh! Stop with the dialogue. Just give us the music and the dancing!"

Dirty Dancing provided the soundtrack of my high school years, with ridiculously fun music, but the movie was not cinema storytelling at its finest. We didn't take it seriously back then and it was more of a beloved joke we liked to tell, like Valentine's Day. We didn't watch it for the story. It was all about the music and dancing.

This stage show was bizarre in that they worked hard to cast people who looked like the stars of the original movie. The actor playing the male lead sort of looked and sounded exactly like Patrick Swayze and the girl playing "Baby," the female lead, was touted as a "newcomer" because she was obviously only cast for her frizzy hair and large nose (Jennifer Grey was the original girl and spent lots of money to get rid of this iconic nose and render herself unrecognizable).

With a mix of video backdrops and a limited set, they faithfully attempted to recreate all of the movie's iconic scenes. Occasionally, one of the chorus people would break into song and sing a piece from the film's soundtrack. In a word, it was bizarre. Interestingly, Philippe had never seen the movie so he was left to decipher the "classic story" without the benefit of the original. His verdict was that it was sort of interesting and he liked the leggy blond girl because she looked like an improved version of Lady Gaga.

But like the movie, the stage show sort of kept you watching and wondering what might happen next, all without the extra bother of being remotely invested in any of the characters. For those who don't know the story, it's about a rich, homely girl who tries learning to dance, falls for her dance instructor from the wrong side of the tracks, all while helping another dance instructor through a botched abortion. No seriously, that's the entire plot, set in the 1960's with a definitively 1980's soundtrack. Sorry, should have prefaced that one with a spoiler alert warning.

Though I wouldn't say we had the time of our lives, it was certainly something interesting to do for the evening. Not something I'd probably see again. But, if you liked the movie, have absolutely nothing else to do with your evening, and are given free tickets, then I highly recommend it.

LOST IN A SONG

There's really nothing better than listening to great music. Everyone has their own tastes, to be sure, but one thing is certain. There's really nothing better than hearing a *favorite* song. Or, at least, my favorite song these days, as my tastes tend to change quite a lot. When I was young, I listened to the radio while driving and still remember the thrill when a favorite song began to play. Or, I'd play a CD and keep hitting the same track over and over again until I had it memorized properly. Not just the words, but every beat of emotion in it.

There would be songs that I played when I was happy and energized that fit that mood and filled me with additional electricity. But, I also loved sad songs, that comforted me. Not by telling me life was fine, but by confirming it sucks in precisely the same way I was currently imagining it did. A song knows better than to try to cheer you up when you're perfectly ready to wallow in a bit of sadness. And yet, still manages to make you happy about everything in the end.

Though I listened to a lot of pop songs when I was young, I also listened to a lot of songs from musicals. I had dreams of being on stage in a show, which later came true. During this period in my life, I knew all of the popular Broadway songs and would belt them out in my car as I was driving down the road. This would receive looks from other drivers when I'd approach a stoplight at full belt and realize my window was open. Once, I was at the very end of the song before I realized this, and the woman in the car next to me applauded. So, I guess I did it well. Of course, it was more likely in jest, but actors rarely notice or care about that. Applause is applause after all.

On a whim once, I took a trip to Las Vegas to audition for a cruise ship. I could barely afford the flight and thankfully got a deal and a free room from a friend who was a flight attendant. I don't really remember the audition, but I apparently wasn't what they were looking for as I didn't make the cut. It was what happened after that I remember most.

The audition was at one of those casinos that isn't on the main strip. So, I had to take a cab to get there. I was so set on doing that part, that I didn't realize I had no cash to get home until after it was over. As I was leaving, I flagged down an Elvis impersonator (the friendliest looking one of the three that were there) and asked for a ride back to my hotel. He obliged, and I was immediately thankful. That was, until I realized he couldn't break character.

The entire trip back, he continued to pretend to actually *be* Elvis. The fatter, older one, for those more visual. It was a short trip that seemed to take an eternity, but I was thankfully dropped off at my hotel and not taken to a creepy tour bus in the desert. As I was getting out of the car, Elvis said, "Ambition is a dream with a V8 engine. Do something worth remembering." I simply nodded, thanked him, and rushed back into the hotel. Later, in my room, I thought about the adventure I had blindly embarked upon and realized it wasn't really what I wanted after all. Those were fun days, to be sure, but sometimes, I would simply find myself becoming lost in a song.

WHEN THE MUSIC PLAYS

I'm not entirely sure why I decided to sketch a trumpet, as I've never played a brass instrument. But, I simply felt like painting something shiny in a limited palette. Though I never played this instrument I did play violin in the school orchestra and piano for a few years before getting frustrated that I wasn't getting any better. My real love back in the late 80's and early 90's, however, was performing on stage in musicals.

Besides the singing and dancing that's involved in these shows, which is super fun, I really just loved the ridiculous concept of people suddenly breaking into song. A simple conversation would suddenly get an orchestral accompaniment, and soon, the characters involved would switch to singing into each other's faces. It's perfectly ludicrous. And so, I loved it. I've often thought that the world would be a bit happier place if outbursts of spontaneous singing were to happen in real life.

Songs are a wonderful way to communicate deep emotions. Like those songs I used to listen to in high school after going through a bad break up with someone I can now barely remember. I'd lock myself in my room and play whatever top hit seemed most relevant to my tragedy over and over again. Each time the song played, it felt more appropriate to my situation, though I'm sure, in reality, it was written to express something entirely different. In the end, though there may have been tears, I would always come back stronger and more resilient. There was always a greater sense of hope.

Music has a way of sailing straight to the heart of the matter and songs can use very little words to express entire stories. I can imagine having an argument with someone and suddenly singing passionately about the matter at hand. A duet ensues and though it begins with all of the conflict in the world, it ends with a lovely two-part harmony about, not what divides us, but what makes us the same.

Whether it's a quiet interlude that begins on a piano or the opening fanfare of a trumpet, the melody would lead to the important conversations. At least, that's the way I imagined it. There's so much conflict in the world today that trying to find notes of harmony often seems impossible. Too much dissonance and discontent. But it's incredible to imagine how beautiful the world *would* be if nothing was so complicated that it couldn't be sorted out in a song.

It's a nice thought anyway, even if the world seems quite far from ever being able to sing the same tune.

The improbable fascinates me so I'll just go right ahead and imagine everyone enjoying the same dance. Each step in perfect unison, spinning in a wonderful symmetry that follows each beat and respects every rhythm. A dream filled with those beautiful heartfelt emotions that remove all hate, as we can't help but sway together, in that impulsive way that only happens when the music plays.

THOSE FURRY FRIENDS

I thought it might fun to celebrate all of those furry friends in our life. Most of us have had a pet at some point in our lives, and perhaps have one snuggled up next to them at this very moment. Owning a pet is certainly a bit of a responsibility, but all of the effort is rewarded with what is guaranteed to be a wonderful experience.

Sure, we tend to live a bit longer than they do, so there are times when it's bittersweet. Other times, when it's full of laughter and joy, and then those times of quiet contentment, when everything feels just right and beautiful. These are some of my stories that I hope will remind you of the amazing times you've shared with *your* furry friends.

PLAYING WITH A PET

Certainly one of life's favorite simple pleasures is playing with a pet of some kind, depending on the type of pet you prefer. Although I'm allergic to cats, I think they're super cute, so I've sketched a little kitten. He'd like someone to join him in playing with this ball of yarn, for those of you out there who can do so without sneezing. Kittens always seem to be up for a bit of play.

My own pet, a tenacious basenji, will paw at me to get my attention, just as he's doing now while I'm typing this. It's less of an invitation to play and more of a provocation with a message of, "What you're doing is stupid. Please stop that nonsense immediately and focus on me instead."

If you do so, and attempt to play with him, he'll look at you as though you're crazy. Apparently, you were already playing a game and were just too dumb to realize it. He'll soon just sneeze to express his displeasure with you and wander away to another room in the house. On some days, this inscrutable behavior really makes me wish I had a kitten.

But, of course, it's my dog's unique personality that ultimately makes him so interesting. And although I almost never understand the rules of the games he makes up, attempting to play them is still really fun. The connection with a pet is amazing. Without the benefit or distraction of babbling on about things, you're forced to connect in very different ways. It's such a soulful connection and one that works equally well with two humans, if they're ever able to sit in silence together.

Soon, after all of the games have been exhausted, you'll still find Phineas the basenji curled up next to one or both of us. Despite our obvious shortcomings, he's quick to forgive and happy to receive a bit of cuddling every now and then. And no matter how irritating he was in the moments prior, all is forgotten on our part as well. It's a perfect circle of unconditional love.

There's a lot to learn from the relationship between humans and animals. I've not even begun to understand all of it. A fact that Phineas will definitely concur with, based on his expressions. But I *do* know that feeling love for the simplest of reasons is one of the most rewarding experiences in life. Those times that make us smile and feel a warmth and happiness that words just can't express.

There are always those milestone occasions. The ones with so many incredible things happening that it burns a full story into our memories. But I'm personally an even bigger fan of those tiny moments. The ones you almost miss if you're not paying attention properly. These almost microscopic moments are the ones that stitch the very fabric of our happiness. A quilt of love that makes life far more amazing than it was, even just a tiny moment before.

And so, I've just been told by my furry companion that it's time to bid you farewell and focus on the *very* important matter of playing with a pet.

MY FIRST DOG

My very first childhood pet was a black and white border collie named Misty. When I was very little, Misty was like a third mother to me (the second being my sister), and was always guarding me everywhere I went. My sister is 12 years older than I am, and always will be. A fact I like to remind her of any time we're together. When I was a baby and a young child, she was still living in the same house, and the three of us would often go on walks together. At my age at the time, I didn't walk so much as roll along next to them.

Once when my sister was pushing me around in my stroller we stopped at a store and the sales clerk said, "Your son is so cute!" to which my sister quickly replied, "Oh, he's not my son, he's my little brother." I looked up at her from my stroller with a gleam in my eye, began to mock cry and said, "What? Why would you say that, Mommy?" The clerk looked at her sternly and my sister turned red. Not knowing what to say, she just spun around and simply rolled me away.

Outside we were rejoined by Misty and continued our stroll. Misty always walked very close beside me, sizing up all of the people passing to ensure they were not going to harm her baby. I loved that dog so much, and have such strong memories of her, even though our time together was relatively short.

I remember in our house, there was a flimsy screen door behind the main door leading to the garage. We'd leave the garage door open a bit and whenever Misty wanted to come in from outside she'd pull the door open with her nose. Not being able to negotiate the doorknob, the screen would just swing shut again with a bang, but we'd be alerted to her presence and let her inside. It was potentially irritating for adults, but for a child it was just the wonderful sound of a friend coming home.

This is the point in the story where you could find out that Misty was older and that we didn't get to grow up together. You could also find out about a certain milk truck driver who wasn't paying attention while driving down the street. But that's a story with an ending, and that's not quite how things would go.

Soon after Misty was gone, we were sitting around the table and having dinner. Everyone was unusually quiet as we were all still trying to grow accustomed to the new normal. That's when we all heard it. The screen door inside the garage swung out and made the familiar bang. We froze, not knowing what to think. My mom went over to the door and there was, of course, nothing there.

But over the next couple of years, we would occasionally hear the door and I would tell my mother that it was Misty, or more accurately, the ghost of Misty. My mother didn't believe in ghosts. She was an adult after all. "It's just the wind, Charlie," she'd say and I'd inform her that the garage door wasn't open and ask, "Wind from *where?*"

I just wanted to believe that Misty stuck around a bit. That she just wasn't ready to stop looking after me. And at a time when I should have felt loss and grief, I felt a strange sense of comfort. Sure, it was from a ghost dog, who was now more ironically named, Misty, but as a kid, this just seemed pretty cool. She was still with me, and all I had to do was listen for the sound of my friend coming home.

SPARKY THE HAMSTER

This little guy was named Sparky and he was my childhood hamster. He was cuddly and cute and extremely friendly. He had a rather elaborate system of tubes to play in as well as an exercise wheel, which he never really used, preferring other pursuits like burrowing under the wood chips to hide from people. Sparky and I had much in common.

It's rather difficult to tell if a hamster actually likes you. They seem curious and inquisitive, but less like they care and more like an elderly aunt you seldom see who has completely forgotten your name. Sparky was just so cute, that it really didn't matter. And he seemed to enjoy being held, as he always sat very still and became calm. Now, as I type this, I realize he was probably just totally terrified and playing possum.

One day, I came home from school and rushed up to check on Sparky. I couldn't see him immediately, but this was always the case. I waited for him to come out from his wood chip man cave and meet me for the first time again, but he never came. It was then I noticed one of the tubes had been carefully pulled away and Sparky had made a break for it. I looked everywhere in the house, and even left out food, but he was sadly nowhere to be found. I spent the requisite "feels like an eternity" kid-style mourning period of about 2-3 days before I asked my mom for a replacement.

The replacement came in the form of a new and slightly smaller golden hamster. This one was female. And while I could never quite tell if Sparky liked me, she made it completely clear that she hated me. She had played it like the lonely sweet orphan in the store, but once in my house, she was pissed.

I can't even remember her actual name because I started calling her Satan. She would not tolerate being held and would immediately start hissing and spitting if you tried to touch her. If you thought you could calm her down by holding her, you'd instead find yourself riddled with brown bullets as she tried to assassinate you.

It was less than a week later, and I was still devastated that my sweet little Sparky had gone and left me with a demonic hamster, when I heard a scratching noise. I wasn't sure at first where it was coming from, but I soon discovered it was coming from the closet. I slid open the door to reveal... Sparky! At least, I thought it must be him. His cheeks were six times larger than I remembered them. My child brain was in peril as it seemed like my choices were limited to the now-deformed hamster I loved, or the screaming banshee in the cage. I didn't want either of them!

Luckily, a quick check in the encyclopedia helped me to discover that Sparky's mumps were simply a case of food hoarding, and would go away. Satan's condition, however, wasn't listed, so I assumed she must be covered by the store's return policy. And so, things would soon be returned to normal! Of course now, I see plainly that Sparky had tried to escape so he didn't like me much more than Satan. But, at least he wasn't violent about it.

I never had another hamster after these. And I'm sure hamsters everywhere were breathing a sigh of relief. Even if he wasn't actually fond of me, I still remember Sparky fondly. He's now in a hamster heaven somewhere with all of his actual friends doing the world's largest hamster dance. And Satan is… well… exactly where you might expect.

SOMETIMES, YOU GET LUCKY

Today, my mind went to my grandmother's collie named Lucky. Though he's since moved on and it's been many years since he was playing in the fields of my grandmother's farm, it's a wonderful memory. He was one of the sweetest dogs on the planet and a great protector of little kids like me. I remember that he always appeared to be smiling, and his soulful eyes would stare right into your heart.

I don't actually have a photo of him, so I've had to use references that matched what I remember him looking like. And also, I discovered that collies are ridiculously tough to sketch quickly. I doubt I could capture all of that spirit in a tiny little doodlewash anyway. But as a childhood memory, he's definitely at the top of the list.

As kids visiting a farm, we'd always love to go exploring and Lucky was more than happy to be our tour guide. He didn't simply follow along behind us, but often in front, leading us to the next location he found interesting. We happily followed. Now, as an adult, I realize he was always leading us out of dangerous areas and into places that were much safer. I've no idea how he knew, but he was always figuratively and literally one step ahead of us.

There are so many feelings to express when I think of him, but it's nearly impossible to put them into words that would make sense. I remember taking a ceramics class and I decided I would choose the collie mold and paint it for my grandmother. It was almost comical to see Lucky in the form of a trophy, but also rather fitting. She seemed to genuinely love it as I recall, but grandmothers are good at making you feel that way even if they think it's something awful.

Eventually, the years would go by, and he would start to slow down, until that one visit when we were told that he wasn't coming back again. I remember crying when I learned that he was no longer with us. It wasn't my dog, but it was still like losing a close friend. I've had many dogs over the years and I've loved them all, but some stick in your mind more than others. He was one of those.

And if I close my eyes, I can still remember the feel of his fur and his wet nose pushing my hand back into place to let me know that he wasn't done being petted just yet. He had a quiet contentment and joy for everything around him, even on the most brutally hot summer days.

. . .

CHARLIE O'SHIELDS

I'll never forget him, and will always cherish those memories. Just a little puppy that grew into an amazing and loving creature. You don't always know what kind of dog you'll end up with, but sometimes, you get Lucky.

IF I COULD HAVE A KITTEN

Make no mistake, I think kittens are about the cutest little things in the world. I've always admired them from afar because getting too close results in sneezing and eyes full of tears. Yes, I'm sadly allergic to cats, so I've never had the joy of raising one. My only other known allergy is to mangoes, which feels less troubling. Having a single fruit you can't eat somehow pales in comparison to not being able to cuddle a cute little kitty when you happen upon one.

It doesn't always stop me, of course, as the urge to pet them is simply too great. And as long as I can limit my exposure, I can get a glimpse of what owning a cat might be like. It's lovely! I love the strong personality that seems to say, "Yes, I could totally live without you, but please don't let that in any way undermine the love we share together." In truth, it's likely why I ended up with a dog in the form of a basenji, with roughly the same personality. A bit of dramatic emotional distance, but never wanting to be truly ignored and always up for cuddles, even if incapable of admitting it at times. It just makes me smile to see such independence in a creature that is indeed, in the end, fully relying on us to live properly.

This personality reminds me of my youth, when I grew just a bit too old to be best friends with my mother anymore. I still loved her in exactly the same way, just as I do today, but I was a "big kid" back then and needed to push the limits of my independence. Bless her heart for enduring those years, and perhaps most of the years after. It's definitely part of life, but I wish I'd known back then what I know today.

That each wonderful family member in our lives is really the most important thing in the world. No amount of new friends, new dreams, or indeed grand schemes can ever change that. There's a something else there. A connection, that sometimes can't be described in words. I've forged a life that is often completely foreign to my extended family, but each time we meet, we know, we always share something in common. No matter how different you are, there's always something there that makes you the same. A wonderfully invisible something that you can't always see, but simply feel. That's one of the best connections of all.

And I think with pets, when we happily make them our family, the feeling manifests in a similar way. We notice traits that mimic ours. Little signals that show we're somehow related. Certainly not in scientific terms, as that would be perfectly weird, but in emotional terms. In those tiny moments that make our hearts smile with a joy that proves life is indeed worth living.

Children are the peak of this feeling, of course. In both scientific and emotional terms. A strange replica of who we are and who we were. I've never had a child either. I've just been one, who grew into an adult before he even knew what was happening. And yet, I can still watch my nieces and nephews grow through the same beats in life. Those wonderful learning experiences that make us the person we will ultimately become.

And I hope that I have a bit of wisdom to pass along the way. But, never too much as to block the beautiful failures that make us much better people. I would love to have a chance to nurture those early formative years. To make a positive difference. Perhaps that's why I get a bit teary-eyed in a completely different way when I think about what life would have been like, if I could have a kitten.

DUCKIE

Once, while Philippe was busy creating a wonderful watercolor painting of Corsica, I was sitting next to him doodlewashing a stuffed duck. Meet Duckie. This is the good friend of our dog, Phineas, and you'll always find him like this, unceremoniously plopped on the floor waiting to be grabbed in Phineas' teeth at any moment.

Though this may seem like an odd way to treat your friend, Duckie doesn't seem to mind as his expression stays pleasantly fixed in a blank stare. There's a game that we're meant to play with Duckie as Phineas brings him over to show us, but we've never been able to figure out exactly how to play it. It's bits of tug-o-war and fetch, but the exact order is a mystery and, after a few minutes, he just looks at us sadly because he realizes we must be stupid.

If you're wondering why anyone would doodlewash a dog toy, well, there's a secondary significance to

Duckie. He's the first toy Philippe ever bought for Phineas shortly after they met one autumn back in 2012. I have a fun photo of them meeting for the very first time on Philippe's first night in Kansas City after arriving from Paris. The initial scrutiny would lead to love at first sight and a bond that was unshakable over the next six weeks of Philippe's visit.

After Philippe went back to Paris, Phineas was visibly shaken and sad. Duckie ceased to be a toy and became a stand-in for his newly lost friend. No matter where Duckie had landed in the house, you would find him mysteriously appear again next to Phineas on the couch. He would cuddle up next to him every second he could, occasionally licking him with affection. He did this for a two full months while he waited for Philippe to return.

Whenever I look at Duckie, it brings back all of the memories of that time, which were both wonderful and bittersweet. It's hard to know how to comfort your dog, when you're also sad for the very same reason. When Philippe finally came back, Phineas was thrilled. He immediately ran off to grab Duckie by the neck and bring him to show Philippe. But Duckie was just a toy again now, *their* toy, and it was time for two best friends to play.

With the change in Duckie's status, he soon burst seams and one day while he was once again laying unceremoniously on the floor, he was unceremoniously gutted by Phineas. A sad end for a once prominent member of the family to be sure, but we quickly replaced him with a new one. We've been doing this ever since. You're actually looking at Duckie #10, and he's a spitting image of the first one, as this is the only duck they sell at our downtown grocery store.

When Phineas gets a little too overzealous with Duckie, up to and including attempting to give him a tracheotomy, we simply tell him that Duckie has to "go to the hospital and will be back soon." This worked well at first, when we actually remembered to grab a duck at the store, but sometimes there is a long delay. Phineas just looks at us sadly assuming we must be poor and therefore do not have very good insurance.

But soon, all is restored and we're one small happy family again. And Duckie remains today a symbol of a time when life was uncertain, but love was never in doubt. Although you won't find Phineas cuddled up with Duckie these days. And that's just fine. Instead, he'll be cuddled up next to Philippe, who went from stranger, to best friend, and eventually, the best dad, who, for one little hopeful dog, finally came home.

LAUGHING UNTIL IT HURTS

It's time to celebrate those little moments in life that make us smile and giggle. Those bits that are often so ridiculously commonplace, yet rather humorous when you take a moment to really think about them. Funny times spent with those who share your sense of humor are some of the best moments of all. These are my little observations that I hope remind you of some of your *own* fun memories.

The best bits of life that make us smile bigger than ever before and realize just how wonderful the world can be when we approach it with delight and joy. It's in this state that we're often the most creative. So, I hope you'll smile along with me as I share some of my own giggle-worthy moments.

LAUGHING UNTIL IT HURTS

I once tried to illustrate the concept of laughing, but since I don't enjoy painting people, it made it extra challenging. So, we ended up with this wildly exuberant dog instead. I'm not sure dogs actually laugh, nor do they experience that uncontrollable laughter that leads us humans to fits of tears and stomach pains. But there's really nothing better, so it's no wonder so many people report this as being a favorite of life's little pleasures.

Not surprisingly, "laughing until you pee a little" didn't make the list, as though it's quite similar, it comes with embarrassingly unfortunate consequences. My favorite part of falling into a fit of laughter is that the thing that takes you there is not usually even that funny in the first place. It's just a moment between you, and that friend who knows you better than anyone should, that triggers a comical chain reaction. I remember rolling on the floor with my friend from college, clutching my stomach while laughing uncontrollable, barely able to speak, yet managing to utter the words, "it hurts to be happy!!"

I tend to find humor in absolutely everything in life. This has gotten me into trouble on many occasions. If I find myself in the horrible circumstance of being surrounded by "serious" people, I nearly have to shut off my ears to avoid laughing at something. I usually end up giggling anyway and being shot those horrible serious stares that are devoid of all understanding.

Life, to me, is beautifully ridiculous. Not so much a poem or a love song, but a cherished joke we all love to tell. I can't imagine taking any of it too seriously, and really, what would be the fun in that anyway?

I get this from my family who have giggled their way through hard times, financial problems, and even funerals. There is always something happy to focus on, no matter what bad things are happening in life. Always. It's simply a choice, and you'll always find me choosing happy.

Once, in college, I was completely out of money and found myself unexpectedly crying in the grocery store. The very idea of crying in a grocery was so perfectly stupid to me that I immediately started giggling. I then grabbed those sad ramen noodles I'd been eyeing and headed back to my cramped apartment to enjoy a feast fit for no one. Laughing all the way.

Sure, bad things happen, sometimes every day. But if you look at the world with an artist's eye, you'll always find that the good outnumbers the bad. This, to me, means that life is essentially wonderful and the bad things can't possibly be as important. If I get too stressed about something bad that's happening in my life, I'm letting something small opaque the greater meaning.

Oh, yeah, I don't proclaim to know the "meaning of life" at all. I just proclaim that it doesn't need one. Life doesn't have to be fully understood to be enjoyed. In fact, the mysteries are what makes life so terribly interesting in the first place and propels us to go on living it.

PERHAPS, on that next turn we take around the bend, all will be revealed. So we journey onward, hoping to find the next clue as to what any of this means. And then, just as we think we know *exactly* what it's all about, something really dumb happens and we can't help but smile. Then giggle. Then guffaw. Then, yes, maybe even pee a little as we realize life has told yet another unfathomable joke That leaves us laughing until it hurts.

TRAVELING BY PLANE

When it comes to travel, riding on airplanes can be an adventure in itself. I typically prefer to have my own lovely assigned seat and don't enjoy being cued up like cattle, so I do sometimes avoid Southwest Airlines. There, you have to hope you get far enough ahead in line to avoid getting the dreaded middle seat. That said, if it's still open on a full flight, you run the risk of having someone sit there who doesn't know how to sit properly and oozes into your personal space. This makes flying rather uncomfortable, but at least when you fly Southwest you can always count on some down home honesty from the crew. I thought today, I'd share some overheard conversations I captured on a single flight.

Once, while flying back from somewhere I can't even remember at the moment, I was tired, rushed and bored, so I decided to write a little to take my mind off things. Instead of journaling about my trip, I found myself fascinated with the conversations of the flight crew taking place all around me. It actually started before we even left the ground when the pilot crackled across the intercom with his initial greeting:

PILOT: Hey there, folks. We sure appreciate you travelin' with us today and we'll do what we can to get ya there safely. I apologize for the lack of water on the airplane today in the lavs. The water lines were all froze up! We do have some of that hand sanitizer back there for ya though. So, that should do it.

I made an immediate note to not order anything to drink as there was no way I was going near that bathroom. To top it all off, I was starving and hadn't had a chance to eat anything yet. I got stuck at the very back of the plane and wasn't sure if there was any food left when the flight attendant finally made it back to me.

FLIGHT ATTENDANT: We have two sandwiches left.
CHARLIE: What kind?
FLIGHT ATTENDANT: We're not sure.
CHARLIE: Not sure?
FLIGHT ATTENDANT: We switched caterers… soooo… it could be chicken or it could be tuna. It's kind of mystery meat.
CHARLIE: I'll take them both. And I'll let you know what it is.

FLIGHT ATTENDANT: Yes, please do!

The sandwiches came and were indeed made from some lightly colored canned meat that tasted like neither chicken nor tuna. They just tasted like lumpy mayonnaise. They were incredibly messy and with the water situation, I had no way to wash my hands so I just kept wiping them with a napkin stupidly as though that alone would remove the not quite chicken/tuna smell from my fingers.

As I was nearing the end of the flight, I overheard a conversation initiated by the flight attendant who had served me my mystery meat. This time, she had a captive audience in the form of a woman sitting at the back of the plane who sounded like she didn't want any part of the conversation:

> **FLIGHT ATTENDANT:** You, know, it's really economical to hunt your own meat.
> **PASSENGER:** Oh…Is it?
> **FLIGHT ATTENDANT:** Yeah, and depending on how deer is prepared I can't really tell the difference between that and cow meat.
> **PASSENGER:** Oh really?
> **FLIGHT ATTENDANT:** I had a roommate from California once that said, "Oh my god, you're killing Bambi!" Then I slipped it in her food and she loved it.
> **PASSENGER:** Did she…?
> **FLIGHT ATTENDANT:** Yeah… but when

LAUGHING UNTIL IT HURTS

she found out, she yelled at me and told me she'd kill me in my sleep if I ever did it again… so, you know… I stopped.

Needless to say, I suddenly begin to wonder just want type of mystery meat was lurking in my sandwiches. But truthfully, I was having a blast. These were people who didn't seem to care about the proper thing to say and simply said whatever came to mind and went with it. In other words, they were my people.

As I type this now, having no clue what I'm going to say next and not really editing what comes out, I appreciate this flight crew all the more. Saying what comes to mind and just being yourself is never really a bad thing. In fact, it can make a rather stressful flight somewhat more enjoyable. Especially if you happen to be trapped in the middle seat.

PANCAKES FOR BREAKFAST

I really had no idea what to doodlewash one day, so I decided to share my breakfast. Every Saturday and Sunday our morning ritual includes coffee along with pancakes with wild blueberries on top. Food is deceptively difficult for me to doodlewash. And when you're dealing with blueberry juice, it's a fine line between making something that looks delectable and making something that looks like a pancake massacre.

When Philippe first arrived from France, he made crêpes, but soon discovered the American breakfast was much simpler to create. Granted, our breakfast stops here and doesn't include eggs, bacon, and steak. A mixture that seems grossly gluttonous unless you're running marathons daily or happen to be an actual elephant.

Included on our menu is one serving of some show on Netflix, since we don't have cable. Currently, our show is the Property Brothers, where two twins sell people grotesquely shabby homes and help them renovate them into their dream home. Seeing these "fixer upper" homes is truly a lesson in learning just what some species of the human animal is capable of surviving in. And it's probably not the best choice to accompany food, but we ran out of Family Guy and had to switch to something.

After pancakes, we will often run errands, which includes a trip to our nearby Costco. Timing is extremely important as we don't enjoy crowds and so we try to get there as soon as they open. Costco is a veritable zoo of humanity when you show up at the wrong time.

When Philippe first visited from Paris he was watching people tasting their way through the store and asked, "It's 3:00pm… why are Americans always shoving food in their faces?" Just as I was about to defend my country, a Costco employee set out a large plate of chicken wings as a 6-person family appeared out of nowhere and we were almost trampled in the ensuing stampede. "Oh, c'est pas vrai!" he said, "It's an intellectual misery!"

My first thought was that he would be boarding the next plane for Paris, and I was regretting my decision to bring him to Costco so soon in our relationship. I knew I didn't have much time to get him out of there as there was another large crowd of people forming like vultures ready to attack the pizza rolls, which were about to come out of the mini oven.

As I hurriedly pushed the cart forward to leave, I nearly crashed into a woman in a mobility scooter blocking our exit. She glared at me like a prize fighter to make it perfectly clear she wasn't leaving without a pizza roll. Philippe looked on horrified, and I was left speechless and embarrassed for my country. In desperation I screamed, "Meatballs! Aisle 3!" as the hungry crowd moved in the opposite direction, and we were able to make our escape.

Thankfully, Philippe didn't rush back to Paris, but seeing America through his eyes is always illuminating. I just can't answer him as to why Americans always need to have a drink in their hand ("are they really *that* thirsty that they can't wait until they're home?" he asks). I *know* this country is insane, but it can also be quite a lot of fun. Just like having pancakes for breakfast.

THE SWEAT BEE

I decided to doodlewash something potentially creepy. This time, I tried to capture the likeness of Philippe's arch nemesis. We've enjoyed slightly warmer weather lately and have been able to sit on our terrace at dinner. Unfortunately, we are continually joined by an unwanted dinner guest in the form of an insidiously persistent sweat bee.

The humorous part is that it appears to be just a single bee, though I know it's likely always a different one. Without fail, we'll be sitting down to eat outside and Philippe will suddenly jump up from the table and spin around in a circle waving his arms. The evil sweat bee has returned to attempt to ruin another calm and relaxing evening.

When the sweat bee first showed up to dinner, Philippe would politely shoo it away with his hands as you might anyone who showed up to dinner uninvited. This seemed to work for awhile, but then the bee would return shortly after as though he thought he may have misread the signs and the shooing meant, "Why yes, that chair right... over... there! We've been saving it for you!"

Things took an ugly turn for Philippe and the guest-that-wouldn't-leave when the sweat bee's cousin had shown up drunk on sweat and died on the deck. Phineas ended up stepping on it with his paw and got stung which caused him to limp for the next few hours. Seeing his baby in pain was the final straw for Philippe and the politeness immediately ceased. It was time for this villainous sweat bee to go away... permanently.

The battle began first with an Eco-friendly and, of course, dog-friendly spray. When the evil sweat bee would arrive, one of us was meant to quickly grab the bottle, while the other shielded the wine, and attempt to spray the beast. It was all so dramatic that in my haste to try it the first time, I had the cap backwards and ended up spraying myself in the face. Philippe returned with, "*OH! C'est pas vrai!*" which translates to many things including "No way!", "I don't believe it!", and, in this instance, "I can't believe I married this idiot!"

The spray did nothing to deter the sweat bee who seemed to enjoy the fragrance, so it was time to up the ante. Philippe ran to the basement and came back with a little spray bottle I once bought for watercolor because I thought I might use it one day. He filled it with white vinegar and rushed back outside holding it like an undercover pocket pistol.

When the bee visited, he spun around in circles

spraying vinegar everywhere before stopping to ask, "Did I get it?" As the bee, completely unharmed, buzzed by my face I said, "No, but you did manage to douche the deck." We sat back down to the smell of strong vinegar in our noses, and although the bee *didn't* return, it was a shallow victory because everything we ate or drank now tasted like salad.

The evil sweat bee hasn't returned since that incident so I think the smell was equally offensive to him. Either that, or he flew off to another outdoor dinner party where the hosts were more accommodating, actually *invited* friends over, and were not so weirdly violent.

Perhaps the bee is also somewhere nicer and he can now be found sitting by a luxurious pool, sipping on a sweaty cocktail. He's finishing his last sip and immediately getting angry with a pool boy who's slow with his next drink, holding up his tiny little fists and shouting to the sun, *"OH! C'est pas vrai!"*

MAKING SNO-CONES

Though I may never have gotten the Easy-Bake Oven I wanted as a child, I did get several different ways to create my very own shaved ice delicacies, otherwise known as sno-cones. They seem to be called "snow cones" these days, but back then it was hipper to drop the "w" and form a cool new misspelled word. My very first ice shaving toy was the Frosty Sno-Man Sno-Cone Machine.

The commercial for this mechanical wonder boasted the five different flavors you could serve and showed a boy popping ice cubes into Frosty's head. He then easily turns a red crank, which wasn't easy to turn at all in reality. This made ice crystals spew out of a hole in Frosty's stomach while other little boys looked on, lashing their tongues out at Frosty rather creepily. Yeah, thinking back, commercials were really weird back then. But that was just the beginning, as more amazing ways to make these frozen treats were in my future.

The second way to make sno-cones was the revolutionary Ice Bird which involved a completely different concept. With this little wonder, you got a small red and yellow duck wearing yellow earmuffs. This one had a special container to freeze a giant log of ice. You would then start frantically rubbing the bird on the ice block like you were grating cheese until the cup inside was filled up with ice shavings. You could then take the cup out and add the flavored syrup of your choice. Red flavor was my favorite and featured in the commercial for this one. It wasn't really cherry, just red flavored, and looked more like crude oil on my black and white television. But what it lacked in flavor, it made up for in the sheer enjoyment of making sno-cones with a cute duck. Like so many things, then and now, the process was *so* much more fun than the result.

By the end of the 70's, the ultimate shaved ice marvel was released in the form of the Snoopy Sno-Cone Machine, which is still available today. In this version the ice spewed out of a doghouse rather than the character itself, which is probably why it was more popular. And, by this point, things had progressed a bit and the commercials showed both girls and boys enjoying the wondrous invention together. This machine was really just the Frosty one all over again with a beagle on top, but it was cooler just because it was Snoopy.

It was a blast to create my own edible masterpieces with these things. This was also the closest I ever really came to cooking, probably because I should have received that Easy Bake Oven instead. But, it was a blast to make these frozen treats all by myself and though it may not have been a *culinary* treat like a cupcake or a pie, I still have very fond memories of making sno-cones.

WAITING FOR THE BUBBLE TO POP

When I was a kid, bubble gum was a ton of fun! Though ordinary gum was lovely, back then, a good piece of bubble gum was really the ultimate joy. It had to be a great brand, of course, capable of producing large and sturdy bubbles. My friends and I used to hold contests to see who could blow the largest bubbles. We'd stand in a little circle and shout, "Go!" and the contest would begin. Of course, this was really only the beginning of the fun.

As the bubbles grew and grew in size, expressions of joy turned to mild fear mixed with excitement. Though we wanted our bubbles to grow to gigantic proportions and win the game, we knew that at some point, nearly impossible to anticipate, the bubbles would ultimately pop. All over our faces and hair. In this game, the winner was actually the loser as well. But the hysterical laughter amongst friends really made everyone feel like they'd won in the end. And without keeping score, we'd peel off our bubble faces and have another go.

There are many things in life that feel like this sort of game. Certainly painting with watercolor is similar in many ways. Each splash of paint adds more and more to the page, and there's so much excitement as the image begins to appear. This, yes, is then mixed with just a tiny bit or sometimes a lot of fear that things will go too far and mess the whole thing up. For me, this is not really scary, but actually exhilarating. Just like when I was hanging out with my friends on the playground blowing bubbles.

If everything blows up into a sticky mess, then who the heck cares! Just have a good giggle and jump right back in and do it again! To me, this is what it means to paint like a kid again. I never put pressure on myself to "get it right" the first time because it's only a bit of paper and paint, after all. There's more where that came from, and I can always simply start again. That said, I almost never do. The thought that I *could* try again is enough to remove those silly fears, and I end up happily sketching and painting away and then post whatever happened on that first attempt to my blog.

I don't actually take my sketches seriously. I take them gleefully! It's way more fun that way. And truly, if you're sketching a Slinky or a boy about to pop a bubble, there's really no other way to approach it. But even if you're painting a beautiful bouquet of flowers or a stunning landscape, it's still more fun to lose the stress and just play. The results will always be better in the end when we let ourselves off the hook and just create for the sheer joy of it. No matter what we're trying to make.

Sure, some days, it feels like we made a mess of things, but making messes is part of how we learn. And sometimes, what seems like a mess to us is something other people adore when we show it to them. We're always our own worst critics, so I've learned to just ignore me when I tell myself that something isn't good enough. It's *always* good enough and sometimes rather cool! So, I just keep going back for more and more no matter what. Just like when I was a kid. Life can be terrifyingly fun while you're waiting for the bubble to pop.

WHEN WE WERE KIDS

It's time to take a little trip back in time to when we were little. And while these are stories of mine, I do hope they'll remind you of your own memories of being a kid. Those tender years when life was nothing more than a huge bundle of possibility. So many dreams waiting in the wings to happen and that precious feeling of being practically invincible.

I often access my inner child when I paint and write. He was never shy about trying new things and never worried about making mistakes. And when you're making something new, that's the best possible way to feel! So join me now as we reflect on that wonderful time, not so long ago (at least that's what I'd like to believe), when we were kids.

LITTLE CHARLIE

Today, we're going back in time to the mid-70s (as if the clothes weren't a dead give away). This is only my second doodlewashed portrait (no ink this time, only pencil), but I *did* get the likeness right. For some reason, drawing myself at this age was much easier as it's not quite someone I even know.

In fact, my long term memory is so poor that the only recollections of childhood I have are the stories my mother tells me (and I'm still never sure just how reliable parents are as a source). These are stories we cringe at hearing our parents tell, but since I'm not sure what to write about a selfie, I figured I'd share some with you. Or, according to mom, as I used to say when announcing my 3-year-old self bounding into the room, "Here comes ole Chah-wee!"

The first mom claim involved my learning to walk. I was behind the age kids should be walking on their own and my family was wondering what was taking me so long. One day, I was standing holding the edge of a piano and suddenly let go. I then walked across the room, which caused the family gathered there to erupt in applause. "He was just waiting for the applause," she tells *everyone*, "he's been walking ever since!"

She also claims that I started reading before anyone remembered teaching me. In the grocery store as my mom and older sister were struggling to find the right kind of Campbell's soup (and I mean seriously… maybe that original can is a design that was cool in Warhol's hands, but it was a pain in the butt back before they added photos). I was only 2, but would casually point to the right one each time they were struggling. To which my sister would always reply, "Who taught you to read, Charlie?"

Also, the child you see at the start of this essay, was once asked the million dollar question. You know the one. The mother of *all* questions…

What do you want to be when you grow up?

Funny, how it's so fun when we're younger to dream about possible answers to this, and yet terrifying and impossible to answer as adults. But allegedly, according to mom, I didn't skip a beat and answered, "Famous! So they'll make a doll that looks like me."

Yeah, I'm not sure the validity of these stories as they all sound a bit far-fetched to me, but I have to admire this kid's ambition. Sometimes, I wonder what little "ole Chah-wee" would think of me now. Did

I do all of the things he dreamed about way back then? Would he be proud of "Old Charlie" now or feel like I've failed him? Did I live up to our expectations?

"Sorry, Charlie!" (as that tuna used to say on commercials, making your childhood a one joke nightmare). I don't think I've done everything you set out to accomplish yet. We're not particularly famous now and we never got that doll, buddy. But there's good news, we're still growing up, so we get to keep dreaming.

And I hope dear reader that you're still enjoying growing up as well. And if you still haven't figured out what you want to be or are still waiting to fulfill that promise to your ambitious 3-year-old self, don't worry about it! As little Charlie used to say, "Milk Shake! *Boom! Boom!*" He was just so *profound*, that kid. Always so thought-provoking.

EATING LIKE A KID AGAIN

When I once encountered a drawing prompt of "silly," it took me back to those fun days when my breakfast came in a colorful box featuring a zany and silly character. I loved all of the various cereals back then, but had a penchant for Froot Loops. The colors just made me smile and I used to try to get all of the same color on the spoon to see if it tasted like a particular fruit.

I convinced myself the yellow ones had a unique flavor, but truly, each little loop tasted just as fruity as the last. It wasn't, of course, silly for a kid to eat this cereal, but when I tried to grab some as an adult, Philippe stopped me with that look that kills dreams. I wasn't even going for a full family-size box, as that would be crazy, but tried to get those tiny boxes that come in a multi-pack.

I thought it would be like reliving my youth, one cute little box at a time, but was quickly informed that my youth came with a better ability to metabolize sugar and I needed to put it back pronto. I did, reluctantly, but sulked the remainder of the grocery trip, secretly vindicated that I got to be like a kid again after all.

Our normal breakfast consists of a bowl of oatmeal, golden raisins and blueberries. Don't get me wrong, it's a perfectly delicious and healthy start to the day, but just isn't the same as back then. Not only doesn't it come in a box with a character on it, its mundaneness and normalcy doesn't immediately suggest a fun name or a character sidekick to accompany it. It's just oatmeal and fruit.

I tried to reimagine it in my head, calling it Raisin Berry Oats, but even that sounded too adult and boring. No brightly colored toucan, tiger, elf, or frog would ever agree to be the celebrity spokescreature for *that*. But I fail to see why only food for kids should come with such adorable marketing. For example, I don't adore rice cakes, although they're a healthy snacking option, but if they were marketed as Ronny The Rhino's Rice Cakes, I would happily reconsider them. I don't just miss the ability to metabolize sugar, I miss the fun of food that doesn't take itself so seriously.

So, if you're wondering, this sketch is, of course, from a reference as I never succeeded in getting my bowl of Froot Loops. But, I'm equally glad that someone loves me enough to protect me from even myself. I shouldn't have all of that sugar, but I still miss the memories of those Saturday morning breakfasts, separating loops onto a spoon and watching cartoons. I figured that since Philippe denied me my chance to relive this childhood food, the least he could have done is dress up as a toucan while making dinner. This suggestion, not surprisingly, was met with yet another dream-killing stare.

Oh well, there's more than enough Legos on display in our house to make up for it, I guess. It's not that I don't want to grow old, it's simply that I never want to grow up. This, to me, has always seemed like trading in a wild sense of glee, fun and discovery for a life that's somehow moved on from all of that. Why should we? When I hop in to try something new, which is as often as I can, it makes me feel alive no matter what it is. Even the smallest of daily discoveries can make me feel as though I'm *finally* eating like a kid again.

MY FIRST LITTLE BIKE

Like most little kids, my first bike came with three wheels. I tend to imagine all of my childhood rides in red, but I honestly can't remember the color. What I remember most is the thrill of being able to roll about and go wherever I liked. I'm sure my mother has pictures somewhere of me on the actual tricycle, but all I have now are my memories. I'm equally not sure it was quite as cool looking as this one and was most likely something far more plain and simple. But it wouldn't have mattered in the least.

Getting your first set of wheels is a thrilling occasion. Sure, it really wasn't possible to go faster than the speed of walking, and any child at a run could outrace you, but having those wheels made it all okay. It was a chance to be like those big kids I'd seen on their two-wheeled bicycles as they zoomed past me. One day, that would be me, but in that moment I could dream I was just like them.

From here, I was upgraded to a bike with training wheels. It seemed like a bit of a step backward since there were now *four* wheels, and my entire goal was to make it to just two. Riding on two wheels seemed like magic to watch at the time. It really seemed like it shouldn't be possible. Those kids on 10-speed bikes who sailed down the street on the thinnest wheels I'd ever seen were my heroes. Sometimes, without any hands on the handlebars and always without helmets (this was in the early 70's after all. People weren't ignoring the rules. There were just several hundred on parenting that hadn't been written yet. And we all mysteriously managed to survive anyway).

I eventually got my own bike with two wheels, of course, and could travel farther from home than ever before on an endless number of adventures. This lasted several years and I was initially content, thinking I'd conquered one of life's greatest challenges. But, as with most things in life, there's always something a little better waiting just around the corner.

As happy as I was to be gliding around on two wheels, I weirdly started to find myself craving four again. I had just turned 15 and was learning how to drive something far more adventurous in the form of a car. Well, an old truck my parents let me use to practice. I was about to become as close to being an adult as one gets before actually becoming one. Though who can really say when we actually become one. I would be able to go wherever I wanted with my friends. Not just places in the neighborhood, but places far away from me. I would be able to go on dates and make out in the back seat!

I would soon go to college and have my very own apartment, or compartment as the reality was, but still, it was going to be so amazing. I'd have a job and I would be entirely *on my own!* The independence I sought the moment I was born was just within my reach. Looking back, I only have to chuckle.

We're never truly on our own, thankfully, and life is never better than the version we learn most definitely requires others. But I was so busy shaping *me* back then that I was often too busy to pause and notice. I was on an unstoppable trajectory and great things must surely be happening next! Thanks to those three little wheels of my very first bike.

CANDY DAY

Forget about that diet, put down that carrot stick, it's time to talk about candy. One of my favorite candies is Jelly Belly. Mostly because it comes in an assortment pack, with all of the flavor choices made for you, thus removing indecision and getting straight to the sugary point. Philippe, however, won't let me get the giant Jelly Belly jar at Costco. Not to protect me, but to protect himself. If left unattended, I would likely find the jar empty, and Philippe rolling on the floor, clutching his stomach and moaning, while the dog looks on with his "thanks for not sharing, you asshole!" look on his face.

When I was a little kid, I used to love to go to the bank with my mother. I didn't think that I was going to get any money, nor did I fancy myself a future bank president (I wanted to be famous, after all). No, I went for the candy. And also because, at my tender age, it was not acceptable to leave me home alone, even in the 70's.

One time when we visited, I kept pulling my mother's pant leg (she never wore dresses) to get her attention. "What?" she asked. She was about to approach the teller we had seen last time, and I was determined to stop her. So, I tugged harder trying to steer her in a different direction. "What is *wrong*, Charlie?" she asked. I paused, but told the truth. "I don't like him." She looked surprised and asked why to which I simply replied, "He gives green suckers!"

She said later she was surprised because I had calmly eaten that green sucker without saying a word. Of course I did. It was the only sucker available. But I didn't *like* it. It was green. Red suckers tasted like cherries, orange like oranges, purple like grapes, and yellow like lemons. Green suckers just tasted green. Whether it was a failed attempt at lime or green apple or both, the end result was just an oddly sweet green flavor. I hated them.

Odd today, that my favorite Jelly Belly is green, or at least greenish. I like the pear ones best as they taste like biting into a real pear. Or, at least, a pear that's been petrified in a bath of Karo syrup. At any rate, they're delicious!

We once tried the Jelly Belly *BeanBoozled* game pack which pairs gross flavors with the classics that you eat by spinning the wheel to see what you'll get. It's truly death-defying as you wait to see if yours is flavored as lime or lawn clippings, peach or barf, or my precious pear suddenly made to taste like a booger. Philippe tried two and nearly puked, so it's a relatively short game to try when you have the time.

It's here I always stop and wonder about the person whose job it was to eat 50 versions of booger-flavored jellies and decide that one was the *boogeriest* of them all. I imagine he or she out with friends saying, "Oh man, me too! I was sooooo ready for 5! Haha! If I had to taste one more booger today, I was going to go nuts!" No wait, if this person actually dares to talk about their line of work, it's equally likely they have no friends at all.

Whatever candy you choose, do so with both joy and moderation. Hopefully, you have some candy sitting and waiting for your ceremonial consumption. If it's just after Halloween, you can always ask the kids to share some candy, but keep in mind they've already eaten the best ones. And I think I've already properly warned you of the dangers of playing candy roulette.

RUBBER DUCKIE, YOU'RE THE ONE

Here we have a little yellow duck, which became a bit of a cultural icon with the help of Ernie from Sesame Street and his signature song, "Rubber Duckie." The song actually reached number 16 on Billboard's "Hot 100 Singles" list in 1970 and was even nominated for a Grammy award. It was ridiculously catchy fun for little kids, like myself, to sing constantly until told to leave the room.

For anyone who missed this piece of music history, Ernie sings the song in a bathtub to his duck. It's an incredibly short song with lines like "when I squeeze you, you make noise" and delicious rhymes like "I find a little fellow who's cute and yellow and chubby, rub a dub dubby." Though light on lyrics, not many kids knew all of the words anyway, so they would just repeat the first couple of lines over and over again making the song even more irritating. But the popularity of the song did serve to make rubber ducks the must-have bathtub toy for generations.

But these little guys aren't just for kids as there are also people who collect them. In 1996, Charlotte Lee began collecting different versions of the iconic duck and now has over 5,600 different ducks adorning the shelves of the glass cases in her dedicated duck room. This, thankfully, earned her the Guinness World Record for the largest collection of rubber ducks. To truly enjoy them of course, she'd have to take them to Mumbai, India which boasts the World's Largest Bathtub.

As well as collectors, many artists over the years have fallen for the lure of this duck. Gigantic floating rubber duck sculptures designed by Dutch artist Florentijn Hofman have been spotted floating in rivers all across the world. This, and many other reasons, clearly make this duck the most celebrated and famous bath toy on the planet.

But for me, it was all about Ernie's love song. Without that, it would have just been an odd-shaped yellow duck that squeaked when you grabbed it. The idea of singing your devotion to a rubber toy of any kind is absolutely ridiculous. And that's exactly what made it perfectly awesome! It was so dumb that it made me giggle every time. And so memorable that I can still remember singing along.

Not many things in life have that kind of impact and seeing a rubber duck still makes me smile. Whether it's the size of a small building or just the simple little version I had as a child. Perhaps there will one day be a new iconic bath toy to win the hearts of people everywhere, but for today at least, Rubber Duckie, you're the *one!*

WHEN THERE WERE DRAGONS

Once upon a time, there was a little boy who wanted more than anything to have a little pet dragon. Not the giant, terrifying kind that would breathe fire through its nostrils while scorching villagers. That kind was scary and seemed to have severe emotional problems. No, he simply wanted a tiny one with wings that was small enough to fit on his shoulder or in the pocket of his coat. The ability to fly was crucial as the boy himself had always dreamt of being able to fly.

Once, while visiting a pet store with his mother, he looked in all of the little glass aquariums hoping he'd spot a little dragon to take home with him. When he asked his mother where they kept the dragons, she simply smiled and said, "This isn't that kind of store. Those stores are far, far away in another land, dear. And, seriously, what's wrong with that hamster?"

The little boy simply looked out the window of the

shop, squinting into the distance, wondering just how far that land might be. Tossing and turning that night, he awoke the next morning with a plan. And nothing would ever be the same again.

He quickly gobbled up breakfast and rushed out the door, running as fast as he could to the nearby creek. Walking along the water's edge, he eventually found the clearing with a tiny patch of leaves he'd remembered. Digging into his pocket he pulled out a shiny marble and set it on the ground there. The glint of the sun through the trees caused the marble to sparkle and glow. He jumped behind a tree and peered out at the marble, to see if his plan was working.

Just moments later, he saw what looked like too tiny marbles sparkling nearby only to realize they were actually little eyes! Could it be? He knelt down and crawled closer, until he finally saw a little purple lizard-like face staring back at him. It was just a head peering through the leaves, but he knew it must have wings as well.

It rocked its head back and forth as if analyzing the boy, deciding what to do, now that it had been discovered. The little boy stared back, willing it to fly over and sit next to him. An hour passed, and neither boy nor creature moved from that spot. The sun was setting and the boy looked away only briefly to see that the marble had stopped glowing. When he looked back. His dragon was gone.

The little boy searched the sky, but couldn't find anything but ordinary clouds. And then he suddenly felt very alone. He sadly stood up from his spot, walked over, and reached down to pick up the marble. That's when he saw it! There, in the swirled purple center was a shape he'd not seen before. Turning it just right, he could now clearly see a tiny winged dragon inside. His heart started racing. Had the dragon leapt out of the marble just for a moment and then jumped back inside? It was getting dark, so the boy rushed home, cradling the precious marble.

For many days after, he tried putting the marble in the sun, but the dragon never made another appearance. He carried that marble with him for months, then years, until one day when he looked inside it, he could only see swirls of purple and not a dragon at all.

The now older boy, smiled to himself, as he spotted the much littler boy who lived next door. He walked over and asked him, "Do you believe in dragons?" to which the littler boy nodded vigorously. He gently handed him the marble and pointed to it as the sun caused it to glow and the littler boys eyes grew large as saucers in astonishment. The older boy turned, and started to walk away, but then turned back and quietly said, "Be sure to take good care of him."

LITTLE LIFE LESSONS

As I've spent the last few years sketching and writing each day, my thoughts on life and art have also been captured along the way. For this section, I'm sharing some of those bits of, well, I'm not sure if they qualify as wisdom or just bits of truth. But either way, it's a mix of simple little discoveries I've made along the way about making art and making life itself a more joyous thing to live. Ways to transform even a bad day into a good one! So I hope you'll sit back, relax, and join me as we jump into another round of stories, and enjoy some of life's simpler moments that always manage to reveal those little life lessons.

SHADES OF BLUE

Seeing a drawing prompt once of "shades of blue" took me back to a time when I had a denim jacket, also called a jean jacket. Though it's been around for decades, during the 80's, this was a required costume for teenagers. I had one, of course, and wore it around proudly, often adding buttons for a bit of flare or just to cover the holes that appeared as I completely wore it out. The difficulty with jackets made from jeans is that they don't really pair well with actual jeans, my favorite form of lower body attire. It just looks weird.

This, of course, didn't stop people from decking out in denim from head to toe. There was a term used here in the early 50's for this called the "Canadian tuxedo." This was because of a story where American singer Bing Crosby was refused entry to a fancy hotel in Canada because of his unfortunate choice to wear denim on both top and bottom. Yet, this created a fashion trend that still pops up today. I totally get it.

There's nothing more comfortable than a great pair of blue jeans, so why not wear them all over your body? And blue is a lovely color, so perhaps it's nice, after all, to just stick with it.

I was always behind the trend when it came to fashion as a teenager. Whatever I was wearing, it was almost guaranteed to be *last* year's craze or even something from the previous decade. I was completely behind the times, as they say. Looking back, I realize I just wore what I actually liked. I'd try on all of the fashions that were in vogue, but I wouldn't keep wearing them if they didn't feel like a good fit. I've taken this philosophy with me through my watercolor sketching journey as I try on various artist's approaches and techniques. It's a total joy and I completely recommend it! *DO it!*

Artists should definitely be dipping their brushes in a new way, learning from the masters, and exploring all of the various ways watercolor can be used. But when you find a way *you* really enjoy, stop and take note. There's a reason for this, and when you paint the way *you* love most, you'll always produce something wonderful and enjoy the journey even more (yeah, this works for many things in life, not just painting). And just like denim on denim, it's a bit too "matchy, matchy" to only use *one* style. Mix and match and combine various styles until you find the fit that's uniquely *you!*

And like fashion trends, we can still shift and change as we paint along this wonderful art adventure. But, if anyone tells you there's a "right" and a "wrong" way, this should alert your suspicions. There absolutely *isn't* in art. There are simply impressive and unique ways that artists have touched our hearts over time. Techniques and brush strokes that in themselves create terrific emotions and story. Steal these, and blend them into your own work in a way that fits you like a glove. Or a great pairs of jeans, or even that cherished jean jacket that holds so many memories.

And if you also love painting and sketching stuff! Don't stop! Have fun and play each day to discover those little bits of yourself that you didn't even know mattered so much. The bits that define you as an artist, even if you're just starting out. Our journey is all about finding the artist within and that starts with finding your perfect fit. A bit of flare and fashion, like a well-worn jean jacket, leading you to your next little artistic epiphany, in simple shades of blue.

THE QUILT MY GRANDMOTHER MADE FOR ME

Today, I found myself thinking back to the first quilt my grandmother made for me when I was a kid. I wasn't even sure where it was in the house, but finally found it sitting in the corner of a closet. It's pretty tattered and worn now, with frayed edges and bits of fabric dangling precariously in certain sections.

As I sketched, I found myself gently restoring it to its original state square by square, as my mind took me back to that wonderful moment when I first received it. It's not that I didn't take good care of it, of course. It's simply a natural side effect that happens to childhood things when they are well and truly loved.

The quilt is a delightful cacophony of blaring shapes and colors, assembled in a perfectly random fashion that somehow begins to form back into a pattern. It was crafted from bits of recycled fabric, some from old dresses my mother used to wear and some from items that had simply outworn their original use.

And it was my constant companion throughout my school years, guarding me through the flu and chicken pox while cuddling me through restful naps.

As I grew older, and taller, the quilt grew much smaller. Where once, I could completely cocoon inside of it, I now had to settle for something to drape across my legs. But it always managed to provide the same comfort. It was, after all, still like getting a hug from my grandmother. She lived miles away, but I could always study those patterns and they would take me right back to her. She's gone now, and the blanket has become too fragile to use.

Taking it back out again, all of those memories came flooding back to me. Both the wonderful thoughts of her, but also moments of no real importance at all. Just the feeling of being cuddled up under it on the couch watching some silly show on television. I draped it around me first like a cape for a moment before folding it back into place for this sketch. It's funny how the first memories the quilt brings back to me are only the simplest. Nothing dramatic or indeed eventful at all. Just a warm feeling of comfort that blankets me with memories of love.

I gently put the blanket back in its place in the closet, but the memories are still spinning through my mind. Looking back, I now realize that each time I was with my grandmother, she also gave me something more than my young brain could ever process at the time. She taught me everything from how to pick gooseberries to how to milk a goat. The latter of which I was rubbish at, by the way. But as she was teaching me these skills I would end up never requiring again, she was also teaching me much more. A steady approach to life that comes with an earnest heart and a positive attitude that never falters, no matter what may come my way.

Each moment with her, she added a piece of knowledge that connected with the last to create a tapestry of wisdom that I still hold close to me today. And though objects might bring back memories, I now suddenly realize that, in the end, those wise and wonderful moments themselves were actually the quilt my grandmother made for me.

JOURNEY TO A DISTANT LAND

When I was a little kid, I dreamed of taking a plane trip all by myself to a distant land. It seemed like an exciting and daring thing to do. Though it also seemed a bit scary, I was convinced it could only lead to a grand and thrilling adventure. In my mind, I listed all of the things I would pack in my suitcase for my trip. My favorite clothes were on the list, but none of my stuffed animals as I wasn't certain they could breathe properly confined like that.

In the end, I decided the only sensible thing to do would be to carry along a single travel companion. There was no doubt this would have to be my best friend at the time, a small bear named Buff. This, of course, meant I would also need to pack the matching clothes and pajamas my mother had made for us. But, planning this grand escape in my little mind, only lead to me thinking about all of the things I would have to leave behind. In the end, I never asked my mother for a plane ticket or ever mentioned this dream to anyone at all. Because somewhere in all of that dreaming, I would always realize I already had everything I truly wanted, right there at home.

I would be practically grown up before I even rode on an airplane, but would later get to travel to distant places. What I remember and love about being a kid was that my imagination was so incredibly vivid that everything felt real, almost tangible. Perhaps that's also why I didn't demand that trip. I felt as though I had already taken it. As an adult, I've always tried to get that feeling back. To imagine something so vividly that it begins to burst with color and emotion in my mind.

It's not laboring through "what if" scenarios, but simply mentally jumping into an idea and pretending it's already happening. I've used this technique throughout my career to help me come up with and consider new ideas. And it's precisely why and how Doodlewash came to be. I imagined a place where artists of all different styles and approaches were coming together to share what they made each day. Not worrying over exactly *how* they draw and paint, but simply celebrating the fact that they *DO* it. It was beautiful in my mind, and it's even more beautiful in reality.

When I first started sketching and painting, I imagined that I was already good at it. I knew I had a lot to learn, and would continue to *always* be learning. So, I skipped that bit at the beginning of worrying whether I was good enough to share anything I made. I just started *doing* it. This wasn't born out of anything difficult to acquire like confidence, I'm still working on that, but instead, simply reconnecting with the imagination I had as a child. I was actually scared to go on that plane by myself back then, but that never once stopped me from dreaming about doing it.

I didn't take that flight because it wasn't the thing I really wanted after all. But since that time, when I want something, passionately feel it in my soul, there's never been anything that could stop me from chasing that dream. In many ways, I'm still that little kid, vividly imagining a world of possibilities. Knowing that what I actually do in *this* moment, is the most important step in my journey to a distant land.

LIFE IN JEANS

When it comes to packing clothes for a trip, you'll only find jeans in my luggage. It's the only type of pant I own, and therefore, the only kind I ever wear. But, I do have them in more colors than simply blue to mix things up a bit. They are the only comfortable leg covering I've found, so I abandoned all others years ago.

I once wore dress pants that are sometimes referred to as "slacks," a weird and odd word that should have served as a warning, since they don't fit me properly. The pockets are on the side causing them to flair a bit unless you have no hips at all and are built more like a pencil. This isn't me, so I hate the way they look on me.

I just purchased other colors of jeans, as for some reason, even an event where blue jeans would be deemed inappropriate, a burgundy pair is somehow considered fashionable. This is a distinction that makes little sense to me, but it works, so I've stuck with it.

Thankfully, I don't attend such events anymore because events that come with a particular required attire tend to be boring and drab affairs that I've found are best enjoyed by avoiding them entirely.

In the very back of my closet is the only suit I own, last worn in a wedding several years ago where I was a groomsman. It was actually more of a casual wedding, and the suits were meant to be ironic as they were paired with bright yellow sneakers. This addition somehow made it all more comfortable since the outfit could then be simply thought of as a costume. Since I've only ever had creative jobs, I've thankfully never been required to wear those hideous slacks to work, much less a suit.

It's practically impossible to look creative at a meeting while wearing a suit. It's not attire one typically associates with anything truly imaginative. It's like a bunch of men simply dressed exactly the same, leaving only a tie as the single speck of pattern or color to exhibit a bit of individuality. Jeans, on the other hand, can be paired with any number of tops and fun shoes, which for me, makes them much more versatile. Men's shirts these past few years seem to mostly be a sea of plaid, so this year, I decided to only buy fun prints instead. The last purchase involved a dark blue shirt with leopards and a white one with pink flamingos.

I purchased a tropical print recently, but these are a bit dicey, as there's a rather fine line between trendy and fun and looking like a Jimmy Buffett costume. Philippe assured me it was the former, but after trying it on at home, I still wasn't convinced, so I only wear it around the house. But one thing is definitive. I'm far too old to truly worry about fashion and comfort is king! Life is way too short to spend even a second of it wearing anything that doesn't make you feel perfectly happy. Don't get me wrong, it's perfectly fun to try on different styles when it comes to clothes and even when it comes to art. But when you find that *fit* that feels right for you, it's usually best to follow your heart.

For my daily art, though I attempt the occasional landscape, I'm happiest just sketching stuff that illustrates bits of everyday moments. Simple things that make me happy and remind me of those stories and memories that matter most. And while some may rock the latest fashion and always seem to be uncovering the coolest new trends, you'll find me instead, chasing the tried and true and happily living a life in jeans.

SIMPLE THINGS

When once met with a drawing prompt of "simple things," my first thought was a favorite pair of sneakers. These are actually similar to ones that I own, but I chose to color them orange as I think I might like to have a pair in this color as well soon. Also, I decided to simplify things a bit by only using two colors, blue and orange, which are my favorite two colors. As many of you know, who read my blog posts or listen to my Sketching Stuff podcast, I'm rather enamored with the simple things in life. Objects that aren't remotely unusual, but commonplace, everyday things.

To me, these are among the most wonderful things that life has to offer. Sure, there's always new and exciting things to enjoy in the world, but the comfort found in the little things we love most is unmatched. And I find watercolor so intriguing because two simple colors can become so many more as they move and mix on the paper. And a quick little doodlewash can suddenly become something rather like an actual pair of sneakers, tricking the eye into believing there's more detail there than there actually is.

When it comes to shoes, I used to have more variety. I had dress shoes for work and other occasions, like weddings and funerals, for example, that were made of leather and some even shiny. As I've gotten older, I've realized those kinds of shoes are not the most comfortable. I've heard a phrase that extols, "fashion feels no pain," referring to the fact that one should don any type of footwear deemed trendy and wear it with confidence while smiling through the weepy tears of agony. This just seems stupid to me, so you'll find me instead with a closet full of mostly sneakers.

As it turns out, fashion *can* be painful and there's never a good reason to put yourself through discomfort in order to fit in. The truth is, we're always at our happiest when we're simply doing the things that make *us* happy. It's not really a selfish trait, but more about being true to ourselves. Fashion can quickly turn into a goal to please others and this is never really quite as satisfying as enjoying our own true personality.

Those little quirks that make me feel like I don't quite fit in are actually my favorite things about me. I adore all of the things I have in common with people, but when those things fail to line up exactly, I equally adore the differences. I guess, what I've learned along the way is that of all the things you can DO in life, just make sure you DO *you* and not someone else. When it comes to painting, groups are typically divided into *how* one paints. That's why I started Doodlewash. There, we play with watercolor and/or ink, pencils and other tools and gleefully do so, however we feel like doing it in the moment.

Early on, someone asked me if Doodlewash was a method, and I happily responded that no, it's absolutely not, it's a movement to inspire creativity. And it's also a celebration of art in every style in which it appears. There are no rules, or expectations, other than having a perfectly fabulous time in the process. As it turns out, we all have our own unique perfect fit when it comes to fashion and art. Wear it with pride! It's not hard to simply be yourself when you follow your heart and thoroughly revel in the simple things.

MESSAGE IN A BOTTLE

I once had every intention of sketching a sailboat, but thinking about sailing lead me to think of ships, and then pirates. So, instead of a boat, I ended up with a sketch of an early form of nautical communication that makes the phone with the curly cord look downright high tech. As a kid, I thought the concept of using a message in a bottle to communicate was a bit ridiculous, since the odds of anyone discovering it seemed so slim.

But that didn't stop me from being perfectly fascinated by the idea of *finding* someone's message in a bottle. Now that would have been awesome. Like stumbling on a mystery that's waiting to be solved. Granted, this form of communication didn't exist in the 70's. People actually sent letters. A behavior, which many people today might find just as ridiculous as sending a message in a bottle.

Today, whether we're sailing the high seas or simply taking a European vacation, we can simply text or post something to social media in order to communicate. For example, we can share a picture of our feet on Instagram to prove we're having a fabulous time at the beach and far too lazy to stand up and take a proper photo that might actually interest you. Everything is instantly sent, and instantly conveyed.

Now, receiving something written by hand feels particularly special, but finding the card or note without a reply button makes responding confusing. I'm guilty of this, as though I absolutely love to receive snail mail, I haven't purchased a stamp since the 90's, and this makes sending anything back rather complex and terrifying.

Though we live in an age of instant gratification, I do sometimes long for those days when you actually had to wait to receive a reply. Every word and message seemed to matter more back then. With no delete button you had to actually think about what you were going to tell a person and would work hard to make each word count.

Perhaps that's why I write my posts in a stream of consciousness style. I have a delete button, but I simply choose not to use it. I'm interested in knowing what's really on my mind. Like my art, I don't edit, I just make what comes to mind. I'm much like those people in nautical lore writing messages for whoever might find them. And if you're reading this now, that's so wonderful… you've just found my message in a bottle.

HALLOWEEN HIJINKS

As a kid, I loved the month of October and the countdown to Halloween night. The ability to dress up in a costume and wander from house to house collecting candy was a huge selling point.

My costumes started out with Looney Tunes characters like Sylvester the Cat and quickly morphed into Star Wars characters, since the very first Star Wars movie was released the month after I turned 6 years old.

I've just always loved the spooky fun of Halloween, but am far too old now to go begging for candy. That said, I'm the perfect age to share some bits of lore, silly moments, and fun memories related to my own Halloween hijinks.

SPOOKY SPIDER

I've always been scared of spiders, but during the first Halloween month, when I very first started sketching, I attempted to doodlewash one. As I was finishing it, I started to get really creeped out so I think that was a good sign that I was getting the likeness across. Spiders are just about the spookiest creatures on the planet.

I saw a fake spider today that made me think of drawing one when Philippe and I went to one of those pop-up Halloween shops. We didn't intend to buy anything as we don't intend to do anything special for Halloween, but we wanted to see what was trending. The store was conveniently set up in rows so moving across the store you could shop, sweet kids, bad kids, unoriginal adults, creepy goth adults, cosplay lovers, can't-get-a-date geeks, and party sluts.

I'm always amazed by the vast array of products at these stores and never disappointed by the selection. My favorite are the "clever" couple's costumes. It's all there, whether you want to be bacon and eggs, peanut butter and jelly, or a plug and socket. You're sure to find that perfect costume that's just *so* "us."

Next to these amazing finds were the large fake butts, fake boobs, and the ever clever "endowment in a cast," enlarged to comic portions to ensure you're the life of the party (assuming other equally clever party goers didn't shop the same store) The only thing I ever found fun about going to large Halloween costume parties was watching the people who had waited all year to show off their most juvenile sexual fantasies.

For my costume, I always used the same black cape my mother had made me my senior year of high school when I sang "Music of the Night" from Phantom of the Opera for a show choir performance. I didn't go as the Phantom, but would simply powder my face, add some eyeliner, and say I was Dracula. It was my easy go-to costume and I just stuck with it. I had to watch the amount of eyeliner, as one year I'm pretty sure it was a bit too feminine. It was too late to fix it, so I just spent the evening introducing myself as Dragula.

The only time I ever strayed from my standby was the last party I attended a few years ago. It was the day of the party and a couple of other friends and I were out shopping for last minute costumes. We decided we should all go as sailors under a "Fleet Week" theme, so we went to a military surplus store. Once we had donned our costumes, we looked less like sexy sailors and more like a relatively redundant version of the Village People. It was at this point I decided to simply give up and stop going to these.

HALLOWEEN HIJINKS

So this Halloween, I'll be comfortably at home, and doing my people watching from a safe distance via Facebook. I find this far more enjoyable because I can leave the party whenever I like. For those of you who love these parties, I say, party on friends! I love that you do! But for me, I'm going to once again honor my fears by avoiding all of the spooky spiders this year and putting poor Dragula back in the closet.

THE RAVEN

Once, when I very first started sketching, I wanted to try doodlewashing a skull for the first time. But after I did, it seemed a bit sad all by itself, so I stuck a raven on top to keep it company.

I chose a raven because Philippe and I had been in Barnes & Noble recently and I saw an Edgar Allan Poe book. It made me think of the famous poem. In the story of *The Raven*, this particular guy was perched on a bust of Pallas Athena, a symbol of wisdom, but I'd already drawn a skull, so there you go.

The book I saw was in the Bargain Books section of the store. This is such an awesome section because it includes so many gifts you never thought to give someone and that they never wanted to receive. The kits for learning how to do just about any skill are here for a price that's permanently discounted so you're assured you're giving a gift that never held any real value.

I nearly bought the book I saw, which was *The Complete Works of Edgar Allen Poe* because I was a huge fan of his writing when I was young. The book I had back then was full of illustrations and contained just a selection of his most famous stories and poems. I loved that book and remember it well. This book was a let down because it only had a couple of illustrations and was larger than the annotated King James Bible sitting next to it. An odd pairing to be sure.

I realize now that being a fan of Poe when I was so young was a bit odd. His works are dark and filled with angst and creepiness. He was also quoted as saying, *"I became insane, with long intervals of horrible sanity"* and was found wandering the streets wearing someone else's clothes babbling deliriously just before dying. And, like something from one of his own stories, the actual cause of his death remains a mystery to this day.

When he was found, he taken to the Washington College Hospital, where he died at 5 a.m. on Sunday, October 7. He was only 40 years old, and never became coherent enough again to ever explain what had caused the condition he was in. If any medical records were made, they have all been lost.

Though many have asserted various causes for his death, up to and including a murder conspiracy, we will never know for sure exactly what happened during those lost 5 days that ultimately lead to the end of one of the most famous authors of mystery and the macabre.

Poe created some of the most memorable and chilling stories ever written, and left behind quite a legacy in the short time he was on this earth. And his raven is still one of his spookiest creations.

... And the Raven, never flitting, still is sitting, still is sitting
On the pallid bust of Pallas just above my chamber door;
And his eyes have all the seeming of a demon's that is dreaming,
And the lamp-light o'er him streaming throws his shadow on the floor;
And my soul from out that shadow that lies floating on the floor
Shall be lifted—nevermore!
~Edgar Allan Poe, The Raven, 1845

A WITCH'S BROOMSTICK

As we get closer and closer to Halloween, a witch's broomstick definitely comes to mind. I'm not entirely sure what a true witch would prefer, but I assumed it would be something handcrafted, and since I don't often paint people, you'll have to simply imagine the witch, just out of frame.

The actual history of why broomsticks are associated with witches is fascinating, though potentially vulgar to some. It all started at a time, centuries ago, when people were just learning about ways to create hallucinogenic drugs. Using nefarious ingredients such as hemlock, nightshade, henbane, and mandrake, they would create "potions" that when applied properly could give you the sensation of flying.

If ingested, these potions caused nausea, so it was quickly discovered that a topical approach would work much better. Let's just say that the potion worked best when applied to hard-to-reach areas and so something like a broom was helpful in the application. I'll let you google the actual details yourself, but it provides the link to why broomsticks are still today associated with witchcraft.

By the time the 16th and early 17th centuries rolled around, you would find a preponderance of images that involved witches riding up out of chimneys. But it's not hard to connect the dots with that one. In a stupidly patriarchal society, I would assume many women dreamed of hopping on a broom and flying up out of a chimney. And perhaps this connection with rebellion is what makes a witch one of the most popular Halloween costumes of all time.

There's something fun about Halloween that allows people to challenge the norm and express themselves in totally unique ways. It's a spirit that I happily endorse. And as artists, I think it's one we should always embrace. Most of you who read or listen to my rambles on my blog or podcast know that I'm not a fan of rules that *shouldn't* be broken. In truth, I rather love rules in general as they're the guidepost one can use to know if you're actually trying something different. Rules are great for that purpose, but when they become doctrine I tend to get a little antsy.

We live in a world that's so ready to tell us what we should or shouldn't do. Everyone around us has an opinion, and they're always ready to offer it up as fact. I too have opinions I've now transformed into fact, but I know they're only my *personal* facts of life. Things that I have decided to be true, simply because it feels true to me. I've spent a lifetime wading through ideas and ideals that come my way, and in the end, most of what I believe is almost silly in its simplicity.

I think we're all creative and wonderful beings, capable of magic. Not the kind that scared Puritans, but the *real* magic that can make the world a better place. The kind that isn't so much about spells and potions as much as simply being good, honest, present, loving, and open to new ideas. It's simple, I told you, but magical in practice. And during the Halloween season, the most creepy time of year, it's as close as I come to riding on a witch's broomstick.

PUMPKINS IN THE HAY

I was once trying to draw food throughout the month as Philippe and I were creating our cookbook called *DO Cook!*, but ended up with a prompt of hay. I realize that hay isn't a food item unless you're a horse, but I decided to pair it with some fall pumpkins!

My favorite part of this season is seeing the little hay bales appear outside all of the grocery stores and Home Depot this time of year. Each, stacked with all different kinds of pumpkins. It's a sure sign that autumn has officially arrived and Halloween will be heading our way soon.

Selecting and carving a pumpkin this early, of course, would result in a ghastly mess by the time the day arrived, but very soon that's just what we'll be doing in our house. "We" might be just a bit of a stretch as the dog and I will simply approve the design as Philippe does the actual carving. I'm a bit clumsy and not really good around sharp objects. That's probably why I never learned to cook properly. But I can eat like a pro, and this is my favorite season to do so!

When I was young, I used to go on hay rides. Those were when you went to some remote farm and hopped on a wooden flatbed structure covered in hay bales and pulled by a tractor. Looking back, the entire idea seems a bit weird, but it was really fun to do it in the evening when just the moonlight was shining.

As I got older, the trick in those instances was to sit next to the person you had a crush on as the chill in the air forced the notion of cuddling for extra warmth. I was too painfully shy for that, so I could usually be found shivering alone, just staring at the stars. As much as I longed to be one of those people with a significant other, I felt in that moment, that it was just me and the sky. I can't really think of anything more significant than that. It was incredible.

And the sheer awe of all of those stars, miles away from the harsh lights of the city, is still a memory I treasure. It was like traveling to another world. I felt so small, yet happy, staring up into a galaxy of mysteries that I never usually got the opportunity to see.

So yeah, maybe I didn't have that special person cuddling me back then, but I still had an extraordinary time. I grew out of my awkwardness, and went on to become more cuddly in later years. But, that young boy who didn't quite fit in is still there with me like an old friend. He's the constant reminder that, sometimes, it's okay to simply enjoy the stars alone. No matter how much you want to fit in, there's always something so wonderfully unique about you, that it's not quite possible.

That's why I love filling my world with artists. We get that feeling. We know that though we share a common bond, our styles and approaches are vastly different. And it doesn't matter one bit. We connect on a level that's not so literal. One that's much like staring into a field of stars and knowing they're all part of the same sky.

We're all so unique and beautiful in the midst of a world that can often be common and ordinary. Like stumbling across the wonderfully contrasting beauty that can always be found with pumpkins in the hay.

THE INVISIBLE MAN

I was asked once if I would draw my Halloween costume, but not planning to attend a party, I didn't have one. It was also a selfie art day so I wasn't sure how to combine both challenges into a single doodlewash.

I have many pairs of glasses, but that day, I was wearing the very first pair of glasses that Philippe picked out for me. I figured this might help me solve my dilemma. So I present to you my latest treasure, an extremely conceptual selfie, and my Halloween costume for that year – The Invisible Man.

These particular glasses are special to me because Philippe was still in Paris when he helped me pick them out. At the time, we had no idea that we would ever actually end up together in reality. After sending him multiple selfies of me trying on various pairs of glasses, this pair was his final choice. I figure they qualify as a self-portrait because on justifying his selection Philippe had said, "They just seem the most *you*."

As for being The Invisible Man, now that I think of it, this would be a ridiculous costume were it possible to turn myself invisible. In order to achieve the effect of floating glasses, it would also mean attending the party entirely in the nude. Which, for the majority of parties, is still considered taboo. But I guess since it would be impossible to actually *see* me, I could only offend people who had an inordinate distaste for Ray-Bans.

The concept of being The Invisible Man is fascinating to me, not just for the ability to hide in plain sight, but for all of the questions it evokes. For example, if while attending this Halloween party naked, would it be considered rude of me to sit on the host's furniture? When greeting my friends, would it suddenly seem inappropriate to hug? If someone else decided to attend the party as an *actual* naked person, would my costume be mocked for its lack of authenticity?

These little what-if scenarios that play out in my head are usually what stops me from attending parties in the first place. It's even more exhausting because now everyone assumes after months of not seeing them, that you've been scouring their Facebook page and know everything that's been happening with them. Unfortunately, that's precisely what I *haven't* been doing.

I show up to the party like a clueless fool who's suffering from a terrible case of amnesia. I'm too cheery with Sheila who just lost her father, I smile and ask Joe how he's doing after he was just diagnosed with cancer, and I forget that it's Stephanie's birthday. Even though that was apparently the very reason for this regrettable affair.

In my daydreams, I imagine myself a favorite guest and someone who can happily mingle with anyone who comes along. But in reality, I'm that awkward, uninformed guy who just said the wrong thing. And although, I'm quite thankfully fully clothed, I'm red-faced and suddenly wishing I could just *become* The Invisible Man.

CONTEMPLATING THE MOON

Though I'm fairly sure when I created a prompt of "cats" one October month, I was thinking of the black cats of Halloween fame. But instead, I ended up sketching a random little cat instead. Not quite black or white, but a bit of both. Yet, if you want to apply this better to the season, one can imagine him contemplating a moon. I've been in this dreamy state myself lately, my mind rushing from idea to idea while occasionally stopping, much like this, to sort it all out properly. Just staring into the distance for a moment hoping the answer might shine down on me.

Sometimes, I'm lucky enough for the proper epiphany to occur, but most of the time, it's just a bit of staring into space. Either way, it's a nice way to calm a restless mind every now and again. And when I return to what I was doing, I'm at least a bit more relaxed for having taken that moment. Daydreaming is one of my favorite things to do. My evening dreams are too quickly forgotten, but the ones made during the day always stay with me the most. And if I'm brave enough to pursue them, sometimes, they even manage to come true.

When I was a kid, I dreamed of being on stage. It wasn't the kind of dream one craves for fame or being noticed, I didn't really want that at all. It was simply chasing the idea that I could be someone else entirely for a time. This, to me, was an incredible thing. I loved to pretend I was a different person in a different world. I wasn't trying to escape from any type of bad reality, I was just wanting to experience something totally new. I wondered what it would be like to live someone else's life for a time. To feel what they felt and imagine what they might imagine. To actually dream someone else's dreams for a time.

My own daydreaming paid off eventually when I was cast in my first school show. I was only a nameless member of the chorus, but I approached it will all of the fervor and gusto one might had they actually obtained a leading role. I don't think my character even had a name, but I made one up for him, of course. I can't actually remember now what name I chose. What I do remember is that I took the tiny part I was given and made it into something bigger.

That little success lead to more and more and soon I was a professional actor for a time. Jumping into lives I'd never lived myself in hopes of bringing a character to life. It was an incredible journey and one that I feel thankful to have experienced today. Though I'm not sure I was ever that astounding on stage, it taught me an important lesson in empathy. That ability to understand and feel what another person might be feeling.

And along with this, perhaps one of the most important lessons I've ever had the pleasure to acquire. That everyone, no matter who I might meet, has something to teach me. From that point on, my teachers in life grew exponentially. Everywhere I turned, I could find bits of wisdom and new thinking that I could knit into the fabric of my life.

TODAY, not much has changed. I'm continually surrounding myself with people who can teach me what I need to know. And I'm thankful for each of you who've joined the Doodlewash art community and share your bits of wisdom along the way. I'm in constant awe and admiration most days, often just sitting off to the side, like a little cat, contemplating the moon.

SKETCHING ALL THE WAY

I've been sketching and writing daily from the moment I first began, and for some, this seems either perfectly crazy or an enviable and impossible level of commitment and dedication.

I'm here to tell you it's actually a bit of both and it's enriched my life in so many ways. My goal in all of this is to inspire others to create! Anything at all… and DO it on a regular basis. So if you're not a sketcher, no worries, simply think of whatever creative endeavor you've been dreaming of mastering. The approach and ideas are very much the same. This is my story, but I hope you'll find ways to apply it to your own creative life as I've done, sketching all the way.

WORLD DREAM DAY

As it turns out, September 25th is World Dream Day, which invites us to embrace all of our dreams, goals and aspirations. This made me think back to when I very first started painting, and purchased my very first set of boxed watercolors. It made me feel like a real artist, even if the paints were labeled "student grade." I would go on to learn about richer colors and pigments, but I've never forgotten that feeling of getting that first set.

And I still very much consider myself a student today. But, it was truly like a dream in a box. All I had to do was open it, grab that brush and let those colors come out and play. There's always a lot of discussion on art supplies, but one of the most important sometimes goes unmentioned. And that's passion. It's free, by the way, and doesn't cost a dime. And when you have *that* in your painting kit, you've got the most important art supply of them all. The one that makes dreams come true.

So much has happened since that first day I picked up a paint brush, which was still just a little over 3 years ago now. And my dream back then hasn't really changed much today. I just wanted to make some people smile when they saw my art and hopefully evoke some lovely memories and stories along the way. For myself as well as for the viewers of whatever it was that I posted.

My dreams have come true in so many ways. Thanks to the internet, I was able to connect with people around the globe who *did* smile when they saw my art, and better yet, shared their own wonderful stories that it evoked! And, for my part, I've faithfully shown up each and every day since the very beginning, painting random things and sharing the random stories and thoughts that come to mind. I started a podcast called Sketching Stuff, telling these stories in an audio format. Sort of like a cross between a radio play and an audiobook. Something I wouldn't have dreamed could have happened when I first opened that little box of paint.

It's been an incredible journey and what's more incredible is that it's still happening right now! I have no intention of stopping and, if nothing else, I hope to provide living proof that we can indeed show up *each and every day* to pursue our dreams. Never let anything in the world stop you from chasing your passion. It's the thing that makes us feel the most alive and makes us better people to the people who rely on us. I know I'm always being the best person I can be when I'm true to myself and doing what I love most.

And sure, I have dreams so large and ridiculous that they will likely never come true. But, the very act of dreaming them makes me feel more *alive*. That feeling of being on the edge of possibility is truly amazing. In many ways, just feeling that, fills me with enough hope and wonder to propel me forward. In this state, I can at least do something cool, if not the amazingly wild thing I had in my head. Like simply showing up, to share and write about a little thing I made today. Nothing elaborate, to be sure, but an image of a tiny box of possibility that started me down this journey in the first place. So now, I simply want to pause, smile and reach out my hand to every other person on this planet who will join me in embracing the infinite possibilities that are waiting for each and every one of us, when we decide to embrace the idea of World Dream Day.

MY LITTLE KITCHEN TRAVEL PALETTE

As many of you know by now, I'm not really a travel sketcher in that I don't travel particularly often, so that's most of it. When I first started painting, I got a little travel set imagining all of the places I would like to take it. Then I found out that while I love sketching outdoors, I prefer painting in the quiet and comfort of an interior space. Yet, having an entire studio that takes no space at all is still why I love watercolor most!

I don't need a studio palette because I don't have a studio, and still paint on the edge of my kitchen counter each day. And, since it's a dual purpose space, being able to collapse it all down and set it aside easily is a dream. And when I don't travel physically, my mind is still always taking me on journeys while I paint. I've gone to a million new places thanks to my little palette, so I guess you could say it *is* a travel palette after all!

Getting new art supplies is always such a treat, and yeah, even talking about them is enabling what can often become an addiction. But it's such a fun one! New things in general are awesome, like a new pair of shoes worn for the very first time. But, for me, everything pales in comparison to getting new art supplies. It's like that fresh box of crayons or tub of Play-Doh when I was a kid. I was thrilled then and get the same level of giddiness today!

It's not really the supplies themselves that thrill me. It's that feeling of staring directly at a thousand possibilities at once. It transports me to that glorious "what if list" that I always like to make in my mind. Ideas spinning and rumbling around, filling me with electricity. Like unwrapping a new sketchbook and thinking about all of the wonderful things that are going to appear there. Or, yeah, some of the not-what-I-really-expected things, but, each little sketch is simply another step in the process.

I'm thrilled to be on this art journey and even more thrilled that so many of you are journeying right along with me! Together, we can inspire each other to keep right on painting and sketching each and every day. *Especially* on those days where it seems impossible to do so. It's not always easy to show up each day and make art, but doing so is such an important part of improving and strengthening our skills.

And, sure, much of the credit goes to the support from my fellow artists combined with the simplicity in the way I approach my work. To this day, I'm still doodlewashing with a happy blend of giddy determination, bits of blind hope, and my little kitchen travel palette.

HOW TO BUILD A DAILY ART HABIT

After starting Doodlewash.com back in July 2015, I really wasn't sure where it would take me. I was just incredibly excited about discovering watercolor sketching. Like, insanely excited, and I wanted to share my newfound love with literally everyone I met and hopefully, one day, the entire world!

I'm happy to say that on March 31, 2018, I reached quite a milestone on this journey of 1,000 consecutive days of sketching (including an accompanying story each day!) Yes, 1,000 days of daily doodlewashing (my coined name for watercolor sketching) as well as storytelling (or rambles such as they are)!

I just want to take a moment to thank each and every one of you who have encouraged me and cheered me on along the way. If you're meeting me for the first time through this book, then thanks for encouraging me right now! I also wanted to take a moment to share a bit of what I've learned about watercolor sketching and forming a daily art habit. Because if you haven't started a daily painting and/or sketching habit yet, I think you'd really love it and it's really not as hard as you might think.

ABOUT WATERCOLOR SKETCHING

Watercolor sketching, as most of you know, is simply the act of using watercolor to quickly visualize the world around you. I called it doodlewashing because it sounded fun and less stressful, but it's really the same thing.

You can use only watercolor or mix it with other media, as I do, but the focus is on quickly creating the illusion of something you see, or an idea that's in your mind.

I can barely describe in words the way I felt when I discovered watercolor sketching. It made my heart sing. I didn't have to choose between painting, drawing, or making sketches with pen and ink! I could do them all at once! And I didn't have to worry about making a gallery masterpiece on a pristine sheet of paper. I could just play inside my sketchbooks and make whatever came to mind that day. The illustration shown on the start of this section is just one of the stacks of sketchbooks that I accumulated in those first 1,000 days. I thought about stacking them all up, but the sketch wouldn't have fit onto a single page of my sketchbook.

BOOKS AND CLASSES

The book that started it all for me was a little book simply called *Watercolor Sketching: An Introduction* by Paul Laseau. Well, it really all started with a tree that I quickly sketched, but by the next day, I had completed my first little watercolor sketch from the book followed by others.

While this was a wonderful way to begin and build confidence, I was seeing a lot of folks out there calling themselves urban sketchers and I was intrigued to find out what it was all about. Shari Blaukopf was one of the first urban sketchers I found and I loved her style. She had just launched her first Craftsy class in the previous month and I was excited to take it. So the following day, I launched into her course and created my first little landscape.

Mine didn't look at *all* like hers, by the way, but I happily laughed it off and kept right on painting. I then went on to take lots of other classes that helped inform my style, but perhaps more importantly, inspired me to keep right on sketching and painting.

After just a week of trying, failing and laughing about it, on July 10, 2015, I was inspired to create the Doodlewash Manifesto, a list of 10 do's with absolutely no don'ts, giving me full permission to keep moving happily forward. It definitely helped me get through the tough times, and though it certainly applies to watercolor painting and sketching, it can really be used for most anything at all in life as well.

THE DO'S AND DO'S OF THE DOODLEWASH MANIFESTO

1. **DO** create whatever moves you
2. **DO** learn from the masters, they're super awesome
3. **DO** laugh when your work doesn't look (AT ALL) like the masters
4. **DO** create as much as you can
5. **DO** focus on the peaceful enjoyment and have fun
6. **DO** smile when things don't turn out as expected
7. **DO** something new everyday
8. **DO** support others along the way
9. **DO** try the hard stuff before you think you're ready
10. **DO** & then **DO** some more. Just keep doodling!

WATERCOLOR SKETCHING AND URBAN SKETCHING

Though many urban sketchers use watercolor, it's not a requirement to become one. You can simply head out with a sketchbook and a pencil or any art materials you like!

The key distinction of urban sketching is that it's always done from direct observation, including a bit of context for the scene, to create a true record of time and place. It's incredibly fun and I highly recommend it! My friend Aesha and I decided to give it a go early on, and I discovered that while I love sketching outdoors, I preferred painting indoors. The paint just dried too quickly for the style I wanted to employ. So many of my doodlewashes were quickly sketched live, and then painted later.

Also, I learned that the subject matter that I wanted to practice or paint most, wasn't often what was directly in front of me. This was a side of effect of my desire to write as well as sketch.

I wanted to write about and illustrate my memories and thoughts of childhood, not just what was happening to me right now. So even had I been able to get over my uneasiness with crowds and join a sketch walk, I would have come home with illustrations that didn't fit what I wanted to write about.

| Sketched From Life

So, what did I do? Well, a little bit of everything, of course! You'll still find urban sketches from me, albeit cropped tighter than the usual fare, when it works with the story I want to tell. But not when I'm dreaming of dessert and can't get Philippe to make one for me, so I have to paint those from references or the fantasy of dessert in my mind. (Cue the sad violin music!)

| Remembered Fondly

All of it is watercolor sketching, no matter how it was created, and it's all super fun! Since there wasn't a term to encompass and include *all* of the different approaches, I coined the term Doodlewash to create a space where I could happily include, support, and promote every single one of those approaches and more! So try everything and choose to DO whatever makes you happiest, even if it turns out to be just a little bit of everything! (if you need a name for that, you're a doodlewasher! Be proud!)

MY WATERCOLOR SKETCHING HAPPY HOUR

IN ORDER TO make sure I was able to show up and sketch and paint something each day, the first step was to set a regular schedule. This is not something that is normal for me as I tend to just fly by the seat of my pants doing whatever comes to mind in the moment. But I knew that if I didn't always have the time available, I would be more likely to skip a day, then maybe two, and soon, days would go by without making a sketch. Where was I going to find an hour each day?

Well, the weekdays are busy with work, so I had to give up something I enjoyed to pursue something I truly loved and wanted to explore. I would sometimes join friends for Happy Hour, that time after work where you have a quick little drink and chat before heading home to dinner. I decided to forgo that happy hour and use that time each and every day for painting.

But I didn't become a hermit, of course. That would be creepy. I simply offered to meet my friends for lunch instead. And I soon discovered my new happy hour, was actually the happiest one of all. Yep, I can still have that glass of wine when I like as well, just not much more or the sketches could start to look weird.

On the weekends, I have a little more flexibility, but I still make sure that the plans I make leave me that little hour to sketch and write something each day. And even when the plans don't quite work out, like when I'm traveling and the flight is late, I still make an effort to show up.

Once, while visiting California, for example, I didn't have time to write a proper post and it was nearing midnight, but I was determined to make a 15-minute goldfish before passing out from sheer exhaustion.

So rock that stubborn determination within you and just show up and make something, no matter what!

BUILDING A DAILY ART HABIT

Even when you've found the time and have all of the enthusiasm in the world, there's still a bit of work to building a daily art habit. After the first several months of painting daily, I'd crossed over into something that roughly felt like a happy habit. I literally *had* to show up and gleefully make something each day. I really couldn't stop if I tried. And it even became kind of a fun challenge to make something on those crazy days when it seemed impossible to sneak in a bit of sketching. But I managed to DO it somehow and it was always so exhilarating!

So, what I learned wasn't monumental so much as a reminder of what my heart already knew. I didn't have to worry about what I made or how it turned out. I didn't have to have a specific goal in mind, other than a commitment to showing up to sketch, paint, and practice. I never planned to make over 1,000 watercolor sketches. It just happened naturally. So, basically, I've found there's nothing complex in forming a daily art habit and it just takes three little steps.

STEP 1: PAINT LIKE A KID AGAIN AND POST EVERYTHING

When I started sketching, I was just joyfully drawing, painting and splashing puddles about. I would post my test swatches as art and I was so incredibly proud of them! Release your inner child and stop trying to control what happens next.

Just sketch and paint and have fun and when you're done, you'll hear that inner child shouting with glee, "Put this one on the refrigerator too mom! It's art!!" Too many times, we worry that what we made isn't good enough to post or share. If you made it with all of the joy of your inner child, trust me, it's beautiful. We all want to see it! And, even better, someone out there is really going to love it. Post it!

STEP 2: LEARN WHAT TECHNIQUES AND APPROACHES YOU LOVE MOST

Take all those classes from the masters and join all of the groups you can, but never feel like you have to conform to just one approach. That, after all, isn't what art is all about.

If you love sketching from life most, then do that! If you love that sometimes, but not all of the time, then do both! Wanna sketch first and color later? Go for it! Put on a blindfold and see what crazy thing you'll make? Try it! Seriously, I haven't tried that, but it sounds totally cool, so I think I just might!

The great thing about art is that you never have to actually choose a method. In fact, you'll find that it's simply in the process of trying a lot of different methods that one or, more likely, a combination of several will ultimately choose *you*. That's when you know you're on the path to finding your personal style. And if you don't choose what you really love most, then you won't want to come back to it each and every day. That's why this step, might just be the most important one of all.

STEP 3: MAKE A LITTLE HOUR IN EVERY DAY AND SKETCH

Okay, yes, I said an hour, which doesn't sell quite as well as "Master Watercolor Sketching In Just *15 Minutes A Day!*" But guess what? Though 15 minutes is enough time to make something (just look at that lovely little goldfish I showed you earlier), it's the bare minimum. If you only set aside that much time, then it's far more likely that something will conflict with it and you'll lose that 15 minutes entirely. And end up sketching nothing at all.

But, if you have an hour set aside, even if things get crazy, you'll discover that, as if by magic, time slows, and there's always a tiny bit of time left in the day to sketch and paint.

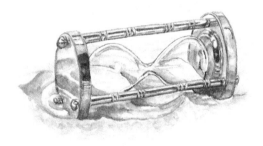

And on those days when you're "in the zone," time will seem to stop entirely, and it's the most amazing feeling in the world!

SKETCHING MY WAY INTO THE FUTURE

It's not always easy to show up to sketch, paint and write each day, but each time I do, I feel like my day always gets a little brighter. And the question that is on my mind and perhaps others reading this: Will he continue to keep up his habit of daily sketching and writing? Oh, most definitely, as it's truly a habit now and I honestly can't stop! Yeah, that sounds more like an addiction, but whatever you want to call it, it will continue.

Sketching and writing each day has enriched my life in ways that I can't always describe properly. It's a feeling that perhaps is best simply experienced. And after all of these days, I still feel like I'm at the beginning of my journey, just practicing and having fun. So if you haven't yet, what are you waiting for? Tomorrow could be the start of your 1,000 day adventure. Join me, won't you? There's a world of things out there ready to be sketched and it's far more fun when you draw and paint with friends!

FOR THE LOVE OF FAMILY

Life just wouldn't be the same without family. Whether it's children, parents, grandparents, and even our pets, there's a beautiful bond there that touches our hearts in a unique and special way.

Though some of my family members are no longer with me, their memories are something I cherish, and I think about them every day. The rest are miles and miles or an ocean away and I don't get to see them very often. But that's the beautiful thing about family. No matter how far away, the connection is always as close as your heart.

WHERE THE WILD FLOWERS GROW

When I was a kid, I would spend many days in the summer on my grandparent's farm. The days would often be so hot and bright that everything was almost burnished to a pure white in the glaring sun. The only thing you could sometimes spot were the various wild flowers growing alongside the gravel road. It was all very different from the manicured lawns and carefully placed flowers of the suburbs where I lived.

These flowers were dotted along the landscape at irregular intervals, and yet, seemed perfectly in place. Nature's landscaping. I would pick a few and take them back to the farm house with me. A souvenir of found treasures plunked into a glass jar for safe keeping. My grandmother had names for all of them. Names that didn't come out of books, but were passed down through the generations, including some that couldn't even be repeated in polite company today. She's no longer with us, but each time I see a collection of wild flowers I still think of her to this day.

It's funny that sometimes the memories we attach to people are not always the obvious ones. My grandmother was far more known for her quilting and I still have cherished blankets that she spent days carefully crafting. This would be a more expected thing to associate, but many of those little squares of recycled fabric also contained flowers. From her perfume to the soaps she kept in the house, the soft, sweet and earthy smell of flowers were a constant.

Beyond that, I remember the intangibles most. Her incredible sense of humor that seemed almost too modern in its uncanny wit and observational insight. She was my mentor growing up, teaching me things that I mostly took for granted at the time. In fact, I think it wasn't until after she was gone that I realized the void. The missing bits of wisdom that I'd come to love so much. Though I was there, holding her hand at the hospital on a few occasions, I was out of the state when she died and unable to return in time to attend her funeral.

There are times in life when we have regrets, those tedious moments that we can't go back and change. I wish I'd spent more time with her in those final days. I was so busy and traveling so much that I could barely spend time with myself. Though I never missed being there for her birthday each year, I often missed many of the times in between. Life would intercede and demand so much of me, making each moment an unbearable choice.

These days, I've learned to take life in a bit more moderation and focus on things that truly matter most. While it's entirely too late to apply this knowledge to my past, it's certainly comforting to know I'm heading into a wonderful future. Perhaps that's why I tend to focus on bits of life that are often taken for granted. Ridiculously simple memories that might be lost if not captured and shared. Moments that often aren't thrilling enough to demand a memory, but always demand a place in our hearts. I've not been to that old farm in years, but I'll always have the fondest of memories, and continually long for those magical days spent where the wild flowers grow.

GRANDPARENT'S DAY

Here in the States, the first Sunday after Labor Day has been declared Grandparent's Day, which is a lovely day for celebrating all of the grandmothers and grandfathers in one's life. I have no living grandparents, and though I've mentioned my grandmother many times, as we were quite close, I would be remiss if I didn't also mention my grandfather. He passed away many years before she did, was rather quiet, and we didn't have a lot of long conversations. But I loved exploring all of the wonders that he had in his tool shed, even though I'm rubbish when it comes to working with tools of any kind, save a pen and paintbrush.

When I was very young, he almost seemed like a superhero with his incredible ability to fix literally anything broken that was in sight. Many times, I wish I'd spent more quality time with him, rather than just admiring him from afar. Tried to get to know him better. But then I think, we had the perfect relationship. The kind uncluttered by too many words that shines with love, even in those simplest of moments spent together.

One of the things I remember most about my grandfather was that he was often a bit impatient with me. He tried to show and teach me things, but I simply wasn't wired to be the type of man that he was. And thinking back to those times when he was noticeably flustered by my inability to work with tools or lift heavy objects, I still have very fond memories. Though I was certainly not a rugged farm boy, he never made me feel like a disappointment or like I didn't belong there. After all of the grumbling, he would just pat me on the back like I'd done something wonderful after all. I would then wander off to play with the goats and enjoy the things that came more naturally to me while feeling amazing.

My hero had once again made me feel like everything was just fine and that through all of my failures I had somehow miraculously managed to succeed. It wasn't breeding some terrible form of false self-confidence, as the grumbles made it clear that I was horrible at doing those things. Instead, I was just given assurance that it didn't really matter after all. We can't be good at everything we attempt, but we should always be rewarded for trying.

These little lessons have served me well as I've grown up and transformed from a little boy into a middle-aged man who's still, most definitely, a boy at heart. I'm not sure if my grandfather ever knew just how much he actually managed to teach me. I certainly wasn't a stellar student at the specific lessons he taught, but I hope he knew that he managed to teach me very important things after all.

Grandparents are often said to spoil kids and give them more leeway than parents might, and I think this is usually true and exactly what needs to happen in life. A person who loves me like a parent, but doesn't have to put up with all of my craziness all of the time, is a perfectly wonderful person to have in my life. They were the first ones to see past those little idiosyncrasies that had already driven my parents to the brink of insanity. The first to let me know that being me was not such a bad thing after all. My parents would lovingly except all of that crazy in the end, but *their* parents always managed to get there first. I have a profound love for my grandparents and hope that, wherever they are, they're looking down on me with a sense of pride. And I'm sending them all of my love and thanks all of the time, making each and *every* day, Grandparent's Day.

THANKSGIVING IN PARIS

Though I love visiting our family in Paris, and adore all of the wonderful French food there, one of my favorite memories is a time we ended up returning there unexpectedly in November. And yet, we still ended up having a full taste of American Thanksgiving. Philippe made green bean casserole, stuffing, mashed potatoes and gravy, along with a peach cobbler for dessert! We didn't have turkey, which I've sketched here, but we did have chicken prepared similarly, so it was a fabulous and mostly traditional meal. It was fun to share a little taste of America with my French family.

And since France seems to truly appreciate food, even the whipped cream in a can, served with dessert, was simply real whipped cream with no cheap alternatives. In other words... utterly delicious! And it was proof that even if you don't celebrate Thanksgiving Day, all you ever really need is good food and family to feel very, very thankful any day of the year.

Since peach cobbler is one of my favorites, it was the food highlight of the day for me. The last time I had it was on my birthday, which also happens to be National Peach Cobbler Day! Attempting to translate "cobbler" was rather difficult because the definition is actually "shoemaker," and so, that's what Google Translate served up first. The dessert we were all eating didn't come until the third definition.

The fourth definition was particularly embarrassing as it's British slang for "a man's testicles" (the dictionary editors bizarrely felt the need to make it clear that we're referring to male and not female testicles). The last definition comes to us from Australia and refers to the last sheep to be shorn.

Needless to say, serving a dessert to my French family that shares its name with shaved sheep and testicles, left me wishing it had been called something else entirely.

Despite language barriers and unfortunate translations, the day was absolutely perfect. Also, while I was there, I snuck in an extra painting for my little niece, Alice, of her "doudous" (which is a French term for little cuddly toys that provide a bit of comfort).

FOR THE LOVE OF FAMILY

I gave it to her and her initial reaction was to look past the picture and make sure her *real* doudous were still there, and hadn't been magically trapped inside a frame. Once she confirmed they were, she proudly went around showing everyone her painting.

These are the moments that touch my heart and remind me that there's so much to be thankful for every day. Those wonderful little moments shared with family are the ones that we remember for a lifetime. I don't get to see my family in France very often so it makes the time spent even more precious. Something so rare that it almost feels like finding gold. And though I may never again enjoy a day quite like this one, I'll always remember fondly that time I unexpectedly had Thanksgiving in Paris.

COUNTRY MUSIC DAY

Grab your boots and guitar and get ready to celebrate some country music! First recorded in the 1920's and originating from the southeastern United States, this music has endured for almost a hundred years. Originally called hillbilly music, it soon became known as "country and western" with singing cowboys like Gene Autry and Roy Rogers creating what music producers considered a more commercial image. Versions such as country rock and country pop developed in the 60's in an attempt to compete with rock and roll. But, part of the appeal of country music is its ridiculous simplicity. It's music born on front porches when someone decided to pick up a guitar or banjo and simply sing whatever came to mind.

My father used to produce country western music shows when I was a kid so this music always reminds me of him as well as my childhood. At the time, I didn't really know or understand the Grand Ole Opry tour bus that was parked outside our home. I just thought it was cool to have celebrities come over for a party! Or, that my mom once baked a birthday cake in the shape of a guitar (for Waylon Jennings, whom I didn't know at all, either, but a guitar cake? So cool!). Suffice it to say, it was definitely the music of my youth.

Though I mostly adored folk music as a kid, there were many country songs that I loved as well. I was actually a huge fan of Ray Charles, so my favorite country song was his version of "I Can't Stop Loving You." Yeah, folk, blues, and jazz were *actually* at the top of my list, but my dad always had a lot of country music playing as well. My dad passed away over 15 years ago now, but I can still remember him choosing music on the jukebox he purchased to decorate his recreation room. He was, like me, a kid at heart. And music was an important part of his life as well.

His brusque manner often made him seem harsh, but I now remember that he would hang on each word of those songs. It was only after his death that my mother revealed to me that he used to read poetry to her. I had no idea, nor would this have been something I could have guessed from him at the time. But looking back now, it probably shouldn't have come as much of a surprise. We weren't really so different after all. And we may not have agreed on the precise musical genre, but we both enjoyed listening for the *truth* in those songs.

As I get older and hopefully wiser, I have fond memories of that time with my dad. Those moments when we didn't have to endure our awkward attempts at conversation, but could just silently and suddenly agree on everything as we enjoyed the words sung by Ray Charles. That's the beautiful thing about music. It's more than words and melody. It's a shared emotion that can be enjoyed by two people who seem to have nothing in common. And though country music isn't my favorite, even today, I still smile each time I hear it.

It's not usually poetic or profound, but simply a celebration of the best bits of life along with the most loved clichés that life has to offer. And though my dad only ever drank beer and moonshine, I raise my glass of wine to him in this moment for a silent toast. I can still hear the music, dad, and I miss you each and every day. I remember each strum of those guitars and banjos of my youth and they always bring back a flood of wonderful memories. A melody of life at its simplest that reminds me of an enduring love. To me, there's no better reason to smile and celebrate country music day.

WORLD KINDNESS DAY

On November 13, 1997, a collection of humanitarian groups came together and made a "Declaration of Kindness" that would become the annually celebrated World Kindness Day. I love the idea of this day which is all about doing something nice for someone, at some point during the day. Simple gestures, also called random acts of kindness, are highly encouraged. Why would something so seemingly simple like kindness require a dedicated day to focus on it? Because, let's face it, kindness is harder than it looks.

Though I consider myself a kind person, it got me thinking about *acts* of kindness. This isn't something you can just sit and think about, it's something that involves another living being. I began to worry because nothing was springing to mind as an example of my kind acts, like helping someone plant flowers (I hate doing that), or helping someone move (that's why they have moving companies), or helping someone paint their house (they're called painters, I'll get you the number).

When someone is sick or in hospital, I hate going because I hate hospitals and the whole situation just feels awkward. I'm horrible with knowing what to do or say and have no idea what kind act I should be doing. I just want to leave. But then I remembered one trip to the hospital I did take before my grandmother passed away.

My grandmother was always a strong woman with an amazing sense of humor. When I arrived at the hospital and saw her, I was shocked to see a frail old woman in her 90's who seemed so scared. I panicked wondering what the "kind" people would do and say in this situation. I should have brought flowers, or a card, or some lovely baked good or something. But I had nothing.

Then I realized, that being kind isn't done by following a list of social rules to be mimicked. And it's not about doing something that would make *me* feel good. The whole point was this other person, and making them feel like the world wasn't different somehow, even though they're now in a hospital bed. So I walked over to my grandmother and said, "What the hell are they doing to you? You look like crap!"

The scared expression left her face, turning to surprise, and then she managed a laugh. "I know! It's like they're trying to kill me or something!" she said, to which we both laughed. I sat down next to her bed and grabbed her hand. "Do you want me to kick their ass?

Because I will?" I wouldn't. And she knew it. I wasn't one of her ass-kicking kin. But, she smiled at the gesture and patted my hand.

"No," she said. "I want you to sing something for me. You always had such a lovely voice." Then it was my turn to be surprised. I hadn't really known that was something she admired about me. By that point, my sister had entered the room and sat down in the chair in the corner, creating an audience of two. I didn't know what to say, much less what to sing. I was the idiot who came without flowers.

"What do you want to hear?" I asked, to which she replied, "Just something pretty." And so I sang the first thing that came to mind, "On the Street Where You Live" from My Fair Lady, because I'd used it for an audition piece once in my previous life and still remembered it. It's supposed to be a romantic song, which would seem inappropriate, but since it was written in the 1950's, it worked out just fine.

I kept singing songs and holding her hand, as I watched the blood come back into her cheeks and a smile appear. Then I sang some more as she laid back down on her pillow, and slowly drifted off to sleep. I hadn't even noticed the tear that was rolling down my cheek, but I wasn't sad. I had managed to do the right thing, just by doing what someone really needed, and she was happy again.

My grandmother would stick around for a few more years after that, before finally passing away just shy of her 100th birthday. I figured I'd sketch the flowers I forgot to bring that day, even though they were never really required. Sometimes kindness is just showing up, being ridiculously you, and holding the hand of someone you love.

WHEN HE WAS A PUPPY

Though I got Phineas when he was only a year and a half old, he was still fully grown. I'd found him at a rescue and that was their best estimate on his age. Unlike other proud parents, I have no baby photos of him to draw from so I had to use a reference and tweak the eyes a bit to match his. He's actually a brindle, so he probably had a few more stripes on his face, but I imagine he looked roughly like this. Those silly extra wrinkles on the forehead and those eyes that always seem to be asking a question you couldn't possibly answer.

When Phineas first arrived, he was a little terror of energy, running around the house in circles, stopping only to paw at me incessantly until I did whatever it was he wanted me to do. I was never really clear on what that was and most of my attempts were met with a sad little stare that said, "you're stupid, but you're mine, so I'll make the best of it." Many of his looks have always reminded me of kids on a playground who just uttered a dare. He was, and still is, a bit mischievous, but it's exactly why he's so much fun.

Though not technically a puppy, I had to find ways to keep him amused in those early days. One of our games was shining a laser light on the wall so he could chase it. He'd zoom around the room at an impossible speed. So much so, that he'd often have trouble making the turns, launching into one of those leg-flapping Scooby-Doo moves. It was comical to watch and made me giggle each time. He wasn't daunted and continued his circuit with limitless energy, until thankfully, he began to slow a bit and it was finally time for bed.

If there was still a burst of energy left, I would walk upstairs to find no dog at all. Then I'd hear a panting that I swear sounded like a light giggle. This meant we had just enough time for a game of Phineas hide-and-seek. This is the only game he invented that I knew how to play properly. I'd call out, "Where's, Phineas?" and wait to hear more little panted giggles before saying, "I guess he must be gone then." That's when he would wriggle out from under the bed, jump on top, and stand in the middle, striking a pose that a Roman gladiator might choose after winning a fight.

This morning, as he lay at the end of the bed, far older now and less inclined to race around the house, I felt a sense of pure happiness. His youthful panted giggles have been replaced with light snores, and each one makes me smile just the same. Though the tiniest bit of gray has shown up around his eyes, they are still the eyes that I fell in love with. Those quizzical orbs that look at each treat before it's eaten, though it's the same treat as the time before. The same eyes that shift and soften when he wants to be cuddled, but only for a few moments until a better offer comes along or something outside the window seems more intriguing. When it comes to distraction, I can't possibly fault him there.

And each moment we spend together reminds me of the first time he jumped into my lap at the shelter. Of all of our differences, the one thing we had in common was a desire to be loved. And that's the deal we agreed to on that day. Sure, he'll break my heart some wretched time in the future by leaving us far too soon, but for now, I'm content with remembering those wonderful real and imagined memories of when he was a puppy.

HAPPY HOLIDAY MOMENTS

I've always loved December, and counting down the days until Christmas Day was a family tradition I've always cherished. Though thankfully, when I was little, my mom used to have tiny little presents for me that I could have each day of the month, to keep me from going perfectly insane with anticipation. This is the time of year when my inner child literally shoves me out of the way and takes over while giggling and screaming with delight. In short, it's indeed the most wonderful time of the year!

SLEDDING DOWN A HILL

Each winter when I was a kid, I couldn't wait for that wonderful day when there was enough snow to go sledding. The amount of snow had to be just right, as too much would make it impossible and too little would be a horribly muddy experience. I would love to say that I was a pro at sledding, but that would be a lie. I was never able to steer properly and would just point my sled in a direction that looked like it wouldn't maim anyone on the way down, shove off, and hope for the best.

Though I began with a wood and metal sled like this one, my parents quickly switched me to a plastic toboggan in order to avoid lawsuits. The plastic kind could still topple another child on the way down, but lacked the sharp bits that could slice off precious body parts along the way. The unfortunate part of the plastic version is that you were no longer suspended above the snow and could feel every rock and bump, getting unceremoniously butt-pummeled all the way down. A small price to pay, I guess, for the sake of public safety.

I rather missed the wooden sled as I was able to launch onto it at a run and sail down on my stomach head first. This felt a bit like flying, which has always been a dream of mine. Also, I mistakenly felt that I had a bit more control. Or, I could at least roll to the side should I find myself sailing toward a tree or another child (I would, of course, have the decency to yell, "jump!" while doing so). Certainly, holding my arms out to the side and flapping them like I was flying didn't count as steering.

Switching to the plastic version was a bit of a let down. It lacked the ornate style and didn't feel like a proper sled at all. I think mine was red, and then maybe yellow after the bottom wore out in the first one. Some kids had circular dishes that they rode, but those were simply not an option for me. It was like sitting on a toilet while holding on for dear life, legs in the air, while occasionally spinning like a UFO. You could also sit cross-legged, but I was already too tall to fit properly and could never quite bend my legs into that perfect yogi pretzel.

The hill we always went to was simply called "Sled Hill" and, at my young age, it seemed more like a mountain. I still remember the sheer and gleeful terror I felt the first time I slid down it. Like most kids, scaring the hell out of myself was a delightful thing to do. It takes years to learn how to be *truly* afraid of things. I haven't tried to return to that hill and give it a go, but I've considered it. I'm sure now, it would look somehow small and unimposing, which would sort of kill my life-long memory of accomplishment. I had scaled that mighty mountain, zoomed forth at lightening speed and made it to the bottom mostly unscathed.

In my mind today, whenever I'm facing a difficult problem, I just think back to that time and remind myself that I was once fearless. I imagine myself grabbing that little bit of frost-bitten rope with my mighty mittens and I'm ready to tackle anything that comes my way. Assuming, of course, the problem doesn't actually involve a tree or small children. I really was rubbish at the sport. Instead, I just focus on the bit where I wasn't scared of taking chances and, no matter how steep, I would take the leap and go sledding down a hill.

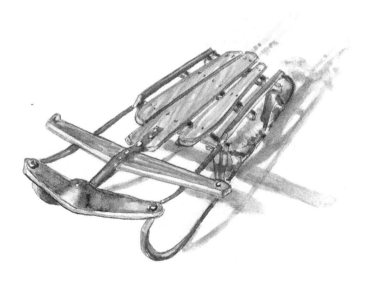

TWO TURTLE DOVES

One of the most played songs in December is *12 Days of Christmas*. It's often sung by adults and children and its repetitive words and melody make it rather catchy and easy to sing. That said, the only confusing part comes when one tries to imagine actually *getting* all of the gifts described. As we sing the song, our true love spends the first eight days giving us a wide variety of live birds. This onslaught of birds only pauses for a moment on Day 5 when our lover surprises us with five golden rings, one for each finger of our favorite hand.

On Day 8-12, however, things take a perfectly bizarre turn, as having run out of birds, our true love loses it entirely and starts gifting *actual people*. Though birds can be seen as pets, one doesn't expect to receive dancing ladies unless drunk in a bar on a 21st birthday. So clearly, our companion is a bit crazy, confirmed by the act of then forgetting each day that we've already received those lovely, odd, and somewhat inappropriate gifts and giving them to us over and over *again*.

This little song has always intrigued me and even as a kid I tried to understand what the heck was going on. Though, at first, it seems we're getting only two turtle doves, by the end of the song, we've actually received a ridiculous 22 doves. In truth, as our amnesiac continues to bestow the same gifts on us day after day, we end up with 184 birds and can only wonder why an aviary wasn't even considered in the list of thoughtful gifts. On the bright side, we did get 40 gold rings that I'm sure might provide enough funds, if sold, to purchase one.

But that won't at all help us in housing the now 40 maids, along with all of the dancers, leaping lords, pipers, and drummers. Though, blissfully, our true love thought about the drummers at the last moment so there are only 12, which probably won't even make enough noise to drown out the birds and 22 pipers. One can only imagine that this song is indeed about true love and that, in the end, it's often *only* the thought that counts.

But as bizarre as this little ditty is, if I stop to question it realistically, it doesn't stop me from joining in the chorus each year. I'll happily hop in with others, singing without care, as we receive a ridiculous menagerie of inexplicable gifts and enjoy each and every one. What I love about this season is that it's rich with traditions that don't always make perfect sense. Songs and stories that are enjoyed over and over again with glee, never stopping to question why.

It's a magical time of doing things that generations

before us did as well. In this way, we're all reconnected to our wonderful present life and a life long before us filled with equal bits of good cheer. That, to me, is the greatest gift of the year. It's one you don't open with your hands, but simply with your heart. A moment of love, hope and joy that can start with something as oddly simple as a single partridge and two turtle doves.

MEN IN BOOTS

While I do love winter snow, I've never been a fan of wearing boots. This doodlewash is of the only pair I actually own and they've only been worn a few times. These I bought after I realized just how freaking cold it can get in Montréal, Canada. I had gone there for the first time to scout locations for a Christmas movie I was working on for the Hallmark Channel. The movie was about Santa's home town, so snow was required, but I somehow didn't realize we'd actually be trudging through the stuff during the trip. I had worn regular shoes and found myself knee deep in snow at one point.

The others giggled at my lack of preparedness and kept asking if I was okay. Not wanting to seem like a total idiot, I said I was fine. I actually was at that moment, since I couldn't feel my feet at all, so they really weren't a bother. It was heading back to the hotel, when I *still* couldn't feel my feet, that I got a bit concerned. Luckily, I was fine and nothing had to be chopped off, but I returned on the next visit with these boots instead. Though faux fur-lined and visually cozy, they proved to be little help against the bitter cold, but this time, since I at least looked the part, nobody asked questions.

These were found online and, while I was shopping for boots, the first thing I realized was that most were perfectly ugly. They were all large clunky bricks that I couldn't bear to wear, so I opted for these because they sort of looked a bit more like actual footwear. There are many men who look perfectly sexy and rugged in a pair of bulky books. I, however, am not one of them. Instead, I look more like a child who tried on his father's boots for a bit of play. Sure, I guess if I managed to complete the outfit with loose, washed out jeans, a heavy flannel plaid shirt, and one of those furry caps with ear coverings, it might help.

Unfortunately, I don't own anything like that as I don't live in the wilderness fearing the next bear attack or drive a truck. While growing up, I quickly learned that I wasn't "a man's man," or at least in the disappointing way I discovered that it meant. To be this kind of man meant you were a guy who loves to prowl around in man packs, go camping, and do manly things. I was never taken on those camping trips, most likely because I asked if there would be appropriate light for reading and if I should bring my violin.

I was only briefly in Boy Scouts, when a neighbor boy who was popular at school joined and I thought it might help me seem cooler. Well it was actually Cub

Scouts as I was apparently too young to be considered a boy and instead seen more as a baby carnivorous mammal. The most exciting bit was getting to build a wooden car for the event known as the pinewood derby. The official car kit came with a rectangular block of wood, four wheels, and four nails. I was thrilled at the infinite possibilities and immediately began sketching designs and making color swatches.

My car was a vision in bright orange in homage to the show *The Dukes of Hazzard*, and to my wee little eyes, looked like a winner. Unfortunately, I'd whittled most of the block away and the car was too light to roll properly. One is allowed to stick pennies or drill some lead in I believe, but that would have messed up my aesthetic. It rolled so slowly down the ramp, I actually caught some of the other cubs yawning. Shortly after, I quit the Scouts, and joined a ceramics class instead. I was the only boy, but I didn't care. By then it was perfectly clear that I was just never meant be one of those men in boots.

SILVER BELLS

One of the signature sounds of the holiday season is the song, *Silver Bells*. In its original form, this is one of the slowest, dreariest Christmas songs that is played each year. The song is set at a tempo that makes it sound as if someone bumped into an old record player and accidentally changed the speed. You keep anticipating the next phrase, but it fails to come in a timely fashion, and rather than feeling joy, you just feel like you want to curl up and have a nap.

I far prefer the uptempo sounds of Brenda Lee's *Jingle Bell Rock*. Also, this was the song that was playing the first time Philippe and I met in Chicago, so it has a special meaning at the holidays. And Brenda Lee sounds a bit like an elf, so what's not to love about that?!

Actually, we have holiday songs playing as I type this and Silver Bells just came on. I bet I can finish this little essay before it finally lopes along to its lackadaisical conclusion. One remarkable thing about the classics is that everyone sounds as if they've drunk too much eggnog spiked with whiskey. They slur each word and scoop up to try to find the next note in the song, very occasionally succeeding.

Listening to these songs after you yourself have had too much eggnog is a rather metaphysical experience. That's really only happened once as eggnog is far too rich in general to drink in excess. One season, however, my sister made rum balls so strong that a handful would knock you off your chair. Yet, they were so incredibly delicious that nearly everyone had a full handful. That was a rather happy holiday season to be sure.

No matter what music is playing, one thing is certain. This time of year makes me incredibly happy. I'm enthralled at the lights and thrilled by the food. I find each moment amazing and spend a year waiting for these moments to return to me again. It's truly one of the most wonderful times of the year!

And I was right, by the way, Silver Bells just now lumbered along to a conclusion and let us know that, "Soon it will be Christmas Day." Obviously, using a word like "soon" in a song so ridiculously slow is meant to be some sort of irony. But this is, after all, the season of anticipation so maybe it's the perfect song after all. An ode to a holiday countdown filled with excitement for the gifts ahead and the endearing, glittering beauty of those silver bells.

THE GINGERBREAD MAN

When I was kid, there was a fairy tale around this time of year that had the catchy repeated phrase, "Run, run as fast as you can. You can't catch me, I'm the gingerbread man." The rest of the story is macabre and rather pointless, but this line stuck with me. In the common version of the tale, a little old lady bakes a gingerbread man only to have it come to life and run out the door screaming, "don't eat me!"

Rather than have a heart attack on the spot, the old woman just starts chasing him as though this inconvenient thing happens all of the time. He outruns the old lady while mocking her for being slow. Following the old lady, he continues to outrun an old man, a pig, a cow, and a horse. At this point, they've all formed a mob of angry villagers, as apparently even the old lady is still in pursuit. But next, he's quickly devoured by a fox and the story abruptly ends. As stories go, this one kind of sucks.

I've never really understood the point of this tale. As a kid you're chanting along with it and just enjoying the fact that there's so many cameos by your favorite animal creatures. And throughout the race, you're pretty much rooting for the gingerbread man the whole time. His pursuers are trying to eat him, after all, not take him to the zoo. Yelling back at them is well within his right since he didn't do anything, beyond magically spring to life, to deserve to be eaten in the first place.

What's the moral? When someone tries to attack and eat you for no reason at all, just keep quiet and let them? Sure, he was a bit of a cocky jerk, but again, he's the victim throughout the tale. There's no twist. Just a bunch of hungry old people and animals who are trying to kill him until one finally does. The lesson, if there is one, is difficult to decipher.

I actually had to do a fast search online to see if there was indeed some unanimous moral to this story. The most often mentioned motif is that every other character seems to think he belongs to them. This, should somehow teach children that they can't always get what they want. This, of course, falls flat since the fox got *exactly* what he wanted by simply being cunning and also flat out lying.

In the end, the child psychologists seem just as baffled as everyone else and in a last-ditch effort to make some sense of the tale exhaustedly say that the moral is simply that you should not trust anyone without consideration. To me, this is simply proof that this is the dumbest story ever told, and that even the dumbest of stories can often stand the test of time. The point of all of this, I guess, is to say that if you're a fox this holiday season, be vigilant. You might just be able to enjoy a little taste of the gingerbread man.

A SNOW DAY

The best part about winter as a kid was when I realized there was enough snow falling to get out of school that day. The idea of getting a snow day was a cherished event and one of the most exciting surprises of childhood. I woke up to more snow falling while writing this and even though I'm off work this week, it still had the same thrill. I'd been wishing all month for snow on the holidays as it just feels a bit more festive that way.

I stuck with regular wishing, though there are actually other ways to make snow appear, like turning your pajamas inside out and wearing them to sleep. I've no idea why this would work, but it's part of child folklore. A more related way to conjure snow is to place a cube of ice in the toilet and flush it. At least this is related to something cold. Each cube and flush represents the number of inches of snow you'd like to receive in exchange for acting so weirdly. Apparently, you can also put a spoon under your pillow to bring snow, but I can't for the life of me understand the point of that one.

These superstitions are simply updates of the much older tradition of the snow dance, which is another option for the rhythmically inclined. I didn't have time to prepare a proper dance routine, so luckily the snow came without the need for all of those rehearsals. Unfortunately, it also brought bitter cold. That wasn't really on the wish list, so we've been hiding indoors all day. The dog is less amused by the snow and cold temperatures.

When I took him out for his morning pee, he just stopped and looked up at me as if to say, "what the hell is this? Fix it!" I honestly can't blame him, as I wouldn't want to pee in such weather either. Later, when Philippe tried to coax him into his winter jacket, he cowered under my legs and wouldn't come. Thus, stubbornly starting what we refer to as "a poop strike" and running upstairs to curl up on the bed instead. Phineas is now snoring on the couch, no doubt dreaming of being adopted by parents who live in Florida.

But, I'm personally thrilled for a day of beautiful snow and lots of time to play with Christmas toys. Or, as is more accurately the case, bounce from one thing to the next and then look at the clock wondering where all of the time has gone. I spent so much time just mindlessly doodling today, that I almost didn't have time write or sketch anything. That's the sign of a snow day well spent, in my opinion. Just a bit of goofing off and not taking life too seriously. Though, I tend to live most days of my life that way.

HAPPY HOLIDAY MOMENTS

As the New Year approaches, I make the usual resolutions to be sensible and try to focus a bit more. These are harmless promises I break to myself at the first sight of something shiny and new. It's not that I'm reckless, it's just that I choose to live life with a constant bit of glee. Life is a silly thing to worry too much about as it doesn't last long enough to raise any real concern. So for me, I'll just keep on bobbing ridiculously through it and living each day like it's a snow day.

A LETTER TO SANTA

Though it's been a few decades, dear Santa, I thought I would write you a letter tonight just as I did as a child. You might remember me as the blue-eyed kid with an insatiable curiosity who asked for a purple teddy bear one Christmas. That's likely not enough to narrow it down, but even if you don't remember me, I remember you. Each night, on Christmas Eve, I would leave you some cookies and milk, though my dad always insisted that you'd prefer a Coors Light. I'm not sure why he thought that, but I stuck with milk as I knew you had to drive all night. Well, fly really, which how cool is that?

That sounds like a blast, but I'm sure you get tired of it, just as one grows weary of a morning commute. I hope you know that you brought me a lot of happiness and I know you still do the same for kids all over the world. Thanks for that. The world has changed a lot since I was little, Santa, and it can use extra happiness now more than ever.

There are so many things I wished I'd asked you back then when I was so busy worrying about what gifts I might get. It all seems a bit one-sided and selfish now and I never got to know you at all. But, I guess you're used to that. I won't bore you with the obvious questions you've no doubt been asked a million times. Like, do reindeer manage to make it through the entire flight without pooping? You're not obliged to answer that, though really, it's a concerning thought if they don't.

Nor will I ask why you left the rest of society to live with a bunch of elves, as that's really none of my business. I'm sure you had your reasons. And, of course, I won't insult you with the question of how you manage to fit down a chimney with your impressive girth. At least that's how you've been illustrated. Probably just wickedly assumed because of all of the cookies you must eat in a single night. You could actually be as thin as a rail and have the metabolism of a hummingbird. If that's true, then I envy that bit about you now even more than the flying reindeer.

No, the question I wanted to ask is a far simpler one, dear Santa. What you do *you* want for Christmas? I would have left you more than cookies had I ever known. I mean, what do you get for the guy who makes everything? If I had to guess, you'd want something rather simple, yet something even your elves couldn't make. So, I've made you this little illustration that I call a doodlewash. It's nothing much at all, but it comes from the heart.

As you sail across the sky each year, you probably see a million things that none of us would have ever known existed. You've seen the homes of the richest and poorest children of the world. And you managed to do what many of us often struggle to do, and that's to treat everyone equally. At least, that's how you make them feel.

The simplest gift, after all, is hope. A feeling that can't be wrapped, but glows in each of us as we open every little present we receive. I now have friends across the globe, so if you could manage it, please send them all my love as you sail past. No matter what holiday we celebrate, love is something we can all believe in.

SINCERELY YOURS,

Charlie O.

ABOUT THE AUTHOR

Charlie O'Shields lives in Kansas City, Missouri where he's constantly chasing new dreams, ideas and projects. In 2015, he started a blog to capture little bits of the world in ink and watercolor while writing stories, got super excited about it all, and a popular site, podcast, and global art community at Doodlewash.com was born. His goal is to inspire as many people as possible around the globe to do something creative daily and share their *own* wonderful stories.

- facebook.com/doodlewash
- twitter.com/doodlewash
- instagram.com/doodlewashed

SKETCHING STUFF

STORIES SKETCHED FROM LIFE

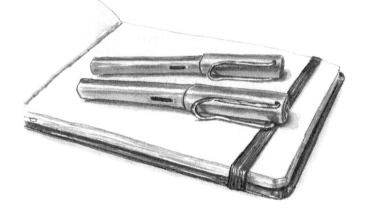

doodlewash BOOKS

doodlewash.com

Made in the USA
Monee, IL
18 March 2020